HAPPINESS

Although happiness is based upon individuals' subjective perception of their own situation, understanding the concept of happiness is important for forming policies in modern societies. Taking into account discussions from disciplines across the social sciences, this book explores varying notions of happiness and how these are applied to create a theoretical understanding of the concept.

The book then goes on to demonstrate how a general theoretical concept of happiness can be used to add to our knowledge of the central aspects of modern society, ranging from questions related to welfare state analysis to evaluating everyday life for individual people. In doing so, *Happiness* presents an up-to-date and applied account of how happiness is now widely used in economics, sociology, psychology and political science, while also exploring the relationship between happiness and public policy.

Bent Greve is Professor in Social Science with an emphasis on welfare state analysis at the University of Roskilde, Denmark. His research interest focuses on the welfare state, and social and labour market policy, often from a comparative perspective. He has published extensively on social and labour market policy, social security, tax expenditures, public sector expenditures and financing of the welfare state. He is regional and special issues editor of *Social Policy & Administration*. Recent books include *Choice* (2010), *Social Policy and Happiness in Europe* (2010) and *Occupational Welfare* (2007).

KEY IDEAS

Series Editor: PETER HAMILTON, The Open University, Milton Keynes

Designed to complement the successful *Key Sociologists*, this series covers the main concepts, issues, debates, and controversies in sociology and the social sciences. The series aims to provide authoritative essays on central topics of social science, such as community, power, work, sexuality, inequality, benefits and ideology, class, family, etc. Books adopt a strong "individual" line, as critical essays rather than literature surveys, offering lively and original treatments of their subject matter. The books will be useful to students and teachers of sociology, political science, economics, psychology, philosophy and geography.

Citizenship
Keith Faulks

Class
Stephen Edgell

Community – second edition
Gerard Delanty

Consumption
Robert Bocock

Globalization – second edition
Malcolm Waters

Lifestyle
David Chaney

Mass Media
Pierre Sorlin

Moral Panics
Kenneth Thompson

Old Age
John Vincent

Postmodernity
Barry Smart

Racism – second edition
Robert Miles and Malcolm Brown

Risk
Deborah Lupton

Social Capital – second edition
John Field

Transgression
Chris Jenks

The Virtual
Rob Shields

Culture – second edition
Chris Jenks

Human Rights
Anthony Woodiwiss

Childhood – second edition
Chris Jenks

Cosmopolitanism
Robert Fine

Social Identity – third edition
Richard Jenkins

Nihilism
Bulent Diken

Transnationalism
Steven Vertovec

Sexuality – third edition
Jeffrey Weeks

Leisure
Tony Blackshaw

Experts
Nico Stehr and Reiner Grundmann

Happiness
Bent Greve

HAPPINESS

Bent Greve

Routledge
Taylor & Francis Group

First published in 2012
by Routledge
2 Park Square, Milton Park, Abingdon, Oxon, OX14 4RN

Simultaneously published in the USA and Canada
by Routledge
711 Third Avenue, New York, NY 10017

Routledge is an imprint of the Taylor & Francis Group, an informa business

British Library Cataloguing in Publication Data
A catalogue record for this book is available from the British Library

Library of Congress Cataloging in Publication Data
Greve, Bent.
  Happiness / Bent Greve.
    p. cm. – (Key ideas)
  1. Happiness.   2. Happiness–Philosophy.   3. Happiness–Political aspects
  4. Happiness–Social aspects   5. Social policy. I. Title.

BF575.H27G74 2012

  302'.1–dc23
  2011018291

ISBN: 978–0–415–68293–0 (hbk)
ISBN: 978–0–415–68294–7 (pbk)
ISBN: 978–0–203–23447–1 (ebk)

Typeset in Garamond and Scala
by RefineCatch Limited, Bungay, Suffolk

Contents

LIST OF ILLUSTRATIONS

Boxes

Figures

Tables

PREFACE

Happiness has been and still is central to many societies and individual persons. It has presumably been a goal as long as human societies have existed on the globe. This book tries to pursue the discussion on what happiness is, and also whether we can measure happiness in a reliable way. The book is written from an interdisciplinary approach, embracing especially sociology, economics, psychology and philosophy, given that happiness is not limited to one branch of research and further that the varied perspectives can help in a better understanding of everyday life as well as goals for societal development.

The book argues in favour of a more nuanced way of understanding present-day societies. Happiness is important. However, the striving for happiness thus also implies that we cannot measure society's development from a perspective using economic data such as GDP per capita alone. We need to include measures of well-being and also how the relations between individuals have an impact on people's everyday life and happiness.

This further implies that political decision makers also should look into how they can help in improving the level of happiness for the individual citizen, as this is important for society's development, but presumably also for their effectiveness and ability to develop in a positive way. The relation between modern welfare states, public policy and happiness is therefore open for analysis. Increasingly, countries seem to be interested in measuring and using the concepts of happiness in order to understand development in different societies. Furthermore, decision makers around the world have increasingly become aware that even though money is important other elements are equally important for the quality of life.

Happiness is a contested concept and some still argue that it cannot be used in social science and political decisions. I hope that after reading this book many people will be convinced that although, clearly enough, happiness research cannot provide us with all the knowledge needed, it will add to our understanding of societies and of individuals' behaviour. It will also enhance our knowledge of why people do not always react in a rational way and just try to maximize individual utility. Furthermore, happiness is not only an individual quest, but society also has a role in maintaining and improving the level of happiness. Increased happiness might even be a win-win situation for both individuals and societies.

Happiness research is here to stay and we can use it in order to develop our society in such a way that in the future we will be able to have stable, cohesive and well-developed welfare states.

Bent Greve
Roskilde
March 2011

1

INTRODUCTION

WHY A BOOK ON HAPPINESS?

This book about happiness is an attempt to present and discuss one of the new themes in social sciences as seen from a variety of disciplines. It is a new theme despite the fact that happiness has been central to people's everyday life for many years, and has been at the core of philosophical discussions of the good society and the good life for centuries. The book will also explain why on the one hand happiness is a new way of understanding contemporary societies, while at the same time the search for happiness has been at the fore since ancient times. Happiness, in contrast to several other aspects of social science, is a topic based upon individuals' subjective understanding of their individual situation in the past and present and in expectation for the future. How a topic based upon subjective evaluation can form an understanding of society's happiness will be discussed. It has even been argued that:

> Happiness became thus a concept attainable for all that could be reached in the here and now. The fact that we can be happy . . . turned happiness into a value of society and laid the basis for our modern welfare state.
>
> (Schimmel 2007: 5)

The book will cross different disciplines in social science and how those disciplines help to understand and make use of the concept of happiness. Furthermore, the book will integrate how one can understand happiness in a theoretical way, as well as how to evaluate and measure it. Additionally, it will examine how the concept can add to our knowledge of central aspects of modern society, ranging from questions related to analysis of the welfare state through to everyday life for individual people. By emphasising the different connotations and uses of the concept, the book will add to the perception of what has an impact on modern societies, and what makes them a good place to live in.

A question that has occupied people everywhere and at all times in history has been how we are, and can continue to be, happy. Most people, at least in affluent countries, are generally happy, although not all the time, and often they can be described as being almost happy. This is thanks to the fact that many are not happy for a long time without thinking about what next new experience, consumer purchase or otherwise, will make them happy. Adaptation is the description of why this is the case. Lottery winners, for instance, are typically only happy for a short time right after they have won the lottery (Yang, 2008). Their happiness will soon fall back to the original level, and this also explains why an increase in income might have a more short-term impact on the level of happiness. Despite this, the search for happiness seems built into human life conditions and is thus also an eternal quest.

A high degree of happiness for individuals as well as groups of persons has been seen as an ideal to try to reach for a good society. The good society is also a happy community, and public action could therefore be aimed at achieving and continuing to achieve a happy or even happier society.

As early as 1776 in the American Declaration of Independence, happiness was seen as central to a community's development. The statement which would guide the development of the USA was built on the quest for happiness as a key measure of a society's development and also for individuals: "That all men are created equal, that they are endowed by their Creator with certain unalienable Rights, that among these are Life, Liberty and the Pursuit of Happiness."[1] Also the French constitution in 1793 inferred that the goal of a society should be general happiness (Bok, 2010: 4).

If the aim is happiness, is it then enough to strive for material wealth? Is the purchase of new flat-screen televisions, cars, clothing, etc. appropriate to ensure that we as citizens and communities are happy? Can money provide us with more happy years? These are just some of the questions that arise if we are to assess happiness instead of looking at the traditional elements of welfare in modern societies, such as growth, unemployment and taxation. Higher taxes might even make us happier (Layard, 2005).

---

1 Here from www.ushistory.org/delcaration/document.

Achieving maximum success and prosperity is seemingly central to most people's lives. We prefer to be happy rather than unhappy. A full stomach after a good hunt could in the past, and certainly presumably also today, make people happy, at least in the short term. A key question is therefore:

How can we be or become happier?

Important issues in modern society are, further:

Are we happier if we work more?
Are we happier if we have a welfare state?
Do we know what it means to be happy?

The problem is that "we" are not fit to find out how or if "we" are happy. It is perhaps simpler to find out that "I" am happy. Individual reviewers can thus be central to assessing whether a family, a city, a municipality, a region of a country, a continent or the globe are happy places. Can we, in other words, measure happiness in a good way? Although we can measure happiness, the problem is whether we can then make societal decisions that make us more happy and enthusiastic than if we did not take these decisions. It is, however, not only societal decisions that are important but also the decisions taken in the family. Decisions and behaviour in the individual workplace also affect how we experience daily life and whether we see life as being happy.

Happiness need not be a uniform dimension that has the same meaning geographically over time, or for that matter within the same family. It is also possible that we do not become happier by having more money, and that happiness can go both up and down, and certainly does over a lifetime. This implies a need for, and an ability to be able to analyse, happiness from various perspectives.

The book's ambition is thus to address the question of happiness from philosophical, economic, psychological and sociological approaches – and thus it presents a new combination and understanding of the concept that is of relevance to modern societies. Furthermore, the aim is to present existing analyses of central aspects of human life and happiness and include data and relations on happiness and core issues of society's development, mainly with a focus on Europe and the USA.

IS HAPPINESS ALWAYS THE SAME?

The discussion of the concept will be more detailed in Chapter 2. However, the question to be raised here is whether happiness is always the same and, if so, whether it is understood in this way all the time. This includes how this can be related to different disciplines' use of the concept.

In some contexts, for example, luck is even associated with something negative – especially in the understanding that being more than happy indicates that the person no longer has a clear sense of reality (Schumaker, 2007). This also suggests that we are unlikely to employ a person who smiles all the time, and also that a smiling judge or examiner does not necessarily give substantially mild sentences or high marks. Happy but naive is another example of how a happy person can be perceived negatively.

Still, there is seemingly a constant quest for happiness and a struggle to become or remain happy. So great is this need that whole industries offering to help people to be happier have evolved. It may be via an adviser (for instance, a personal stylist), self-help books, etc. This is perhaps not an entirely new part of society. Ancient philosophers discussed happiness (see below) and the good life and good society in many books. In 1952, a book was published, *The Power of Positive Thinking*, which sold more than 20 million copies and was translated into 41 languages (Schumaker, 2007). The search for happiness seems thus to be a universal human desire. It is also difficult to answer "yes" to the question, Would you like to be unhappy? posing the opposite – for example being unhappy – over the life but, as will be discussed in Chapter 3, people are able to distinguish between short-term bad luck and long-term happiness. This does not preclude the unhappy moments each person presumably will experience when they have used money in a way they regret, or more directly have lost a family member, or witness some tragedy in the family or among friends.

In the marketing of many products, the idea is often to indicate that you will become happy if you buy the product. What child would not, for example, like a Happy Meal? And which firm would not like to market their products as having the ability to make you happy? How many pubs and restaurants, etc. do not, at least some part of the year, offer happy hours? Here is your luck, seemingly, that it is possible to drink alcohol at reduced prices. A tour around Los Angeles can presumably take one past "Happy Donuts, Happy Liquor, Happy World Baby Clothes, Happy Day Care, Happy Shoes, Happy Trails Pet Services, Happy Couple Marriage Center, Happy Dental Center, and hundreds of other happy businesses" (Schumaker, 2007: 15). All are an indication that the word happy, and being or searching for happiness, are an integral part of our life.

The probability that we will buy a product that presumably will make us happy, at least for a short while, rather than one that does not make us happy, is rather large. Although, as will be referred to many times below, basic needs have to be covered first, and buying bread and water might not actually lead to a joyful life. If we have had a bad experience in a shop, we will hardly shop there anymore, but whether we are happier because the assistants in almost all shops say, "Have a good day" or "How are you today?", cannot be concluded.

There is in some workplaces a Chief Happiness Officer, who must contribute to the idea that "9–5 is Happy Hour" at work. There is a pension company that has developed a happiness meter on its website, which is bound to give customers the impression that having a pension and the opportunity for economic freedom in old age is an important contribution to their happiness. The Happiness Meter also gives instructions on how to live a happy life.

Training programmes for achieving a happier life, and books in the same genre, have also been growing in recent years. Happiness is therefore increasingly important in our daily lives. When it is important in daily life this will also have an impact on society's development.

Religion, as an example, for many people will seemingly – although it might not necessarily be expressed in such a way – be able to contribute to their happiness, and studies also suggest that believers are happier than others. Buddhist thinking, although not all will agree, may be seen as an expression of a desire for everyone to be happy. Buddha has thus expressed the following vision:

Let all beings be happy, weak or strong, up high, middle or lower state, small or great, visible or invisible, near or far away, alive or still to be born, may they all be entirely happy. Let nobody lie to anybody or despise any single being whatsoever. May nobody wish harm to any single creature out of anger or hatred. Let us cherish all creatures as a mother her only child. May our loving thoughts fill the whole world, above, below, across, without limit, with a boundless good toward the whole world, unrestricted, free of hatred and enmity.

(Schumaker, 2007: 102–3)

This explains perhaps why in some studies Buddhists are found to be happier than non-Buddhists, and more generally why believers are often regarded as happier than atheists.

The ambition in this book is thus also to explore and to present what we know about happiness, including measurement and interpretation thereof, and also how this might affect a wide range of fields in individuals' daily life and in the welfare states. The understanding of, and quest for, happiness is socially important because:

Happy people function on a higher level in major life domains such as work, social relationships, and health.

(Kesebir and Diener, 2008: 74)

The significance of this statement is that happy people work more effectively, and probably longer, have better health and more social relations, which especially will be the focus in Chapter 4. This means that not only are employed people happier, but they are also seemingly more effective and spending pressures on the welfare state will therefore also be smaller. It is thus a win-win situation: the individual becomes happier and the welfare state cheaper to operate. Therefore, even if happiness can be understood differently by the individual (cf. also Chapter 3 on whether we can measure happiness), it is important to have an understanding of the different approaches to happiness, and this relates to different life-domains.

DIFFERENT APPROACHES TO HAPPINESS

Economy dominated thinking has for a long time used the utility-maximising individual as the starting point for the analysis and interpretation of how individuals act (Frey and Stutzer, 2002a, 2002b; Layard, 2005). A core problem was how to solve the puzzle of interpersonal comparisons (Arrow, 1950), and how to measure utility (Anand and Clark, 2006).

Knowledge of what happiness is has become increasingly urgent, because many decisions have been carried out with an idea of what creates the greatest possible satisfaction of the maximum number of people. Utility was the term economists used previously, and they preferred to measure it by assessment of "subjective priorities, as revealed in their actual behaviour" (Ott, 2010:1). The core buzzwords here are "revealed" and "actual behaviour", to which we will return in the following chapters. Utility and its consequences have been significant for a discussion of the way people react, and it is used today in much of the discussion of how, for example, different incentives can get people to work more. Therefore, societies might have the risk of taking decisions based on an out-dated understanding of what creates the greatest overall satisfaction. The question of whether happiness has been considered similarly in the course of history will also be included in the book, including analysis of what happiness is and how happiness can be understood from a variety of approaches, inspired by the philosophical, psychological, economical and sociological conceptions.

Whereas economists have focused on utility, sociologists have focused more on well-being and non-monetary aspects, such as the thinking of having, loving and being (Allardt, 1977, 2003). In the OECD, too, social indicators have been seen as an approach that has been able to capture aspects of society's development other than the classical monetary elements (OECD, 2005, 2006).

This understanding of how non-monetary elements and individuals' subjective perception of their daily life have been central to sociological and psychological understandings and use of the concept of happiness, is discussed in Chapter 2. Psychology also focuses on intrinsic and extrinsic aspects of happiness. The movement from elements which can be measured in an objective way to combine objective measures of society's development with the individual's perspective also captures the need for new ways of measuring the societal development (cf. Chapter 5). The problem is also for these approaches to know what is good for an individual (Helliwell, 2003; Lelkes, 2006a), and the possibility that what is good for an individual need not be good for society.

OUTLINE OF THE BOOK

The book has the following structure. After this short introduction, Chapter 2 follows with more focus, and a more detailed discussion, on what happiness is. The work of core thinkers of both historical and modern origin will be used to capture the essence of what happiness is, including why different theoretical perspectives are needed in order to grasp the full meaning of the concept. The chapter also highlights and links the discussion of happiness to welfare, given that modern societies are often labelled welfare states, and, therefore the link between happiness and welfare is important to embrace if one should be able to depict issues of happiness, including the possibility that not only individuals but also societies have a role to pursue (cf. also Chapter 4).

Chapter 2 lays the foundation for the subsequent analysis and presentation, then the more methodological issues are addressed in Chapter 3. This includes whether or not we are able to measure happiness, and the pitfalls and dilemmas related to this type of measurement for the understanding of the results. The chapter also provides empirical examples of happiness, with mainly a US and European focus, for example, on income and happiness, the development in happiness since 2002, happiness and the subjective evaluation of the individual's health, happiness and trust, happiness and hours worked, and social relations and happiness. The chapter will thus use, for example, the European Social Survey and the General Social Survey from the US to present some general findings related to Europeans and Americans and their happiness.

Chapter 4 moves the book towards a focus on happiness and social and welfare state policies. This is due to the increased emphasis on happiness in public debate (cf. for example, a commission established by the French President

Nicolas Sarkozy involving several Nobel laureates (Stiglitz *et al.*, 2009)).

The chapter will look into classical social policy issues such as inequality, the labour market and health, and how they are related to happiness. Can we, for example, expect to live longer if we are able to create a happy society? Happiness and social relations are also discussed and the relation to income and the Easterlin hypothesis is presented.

Furthermore, using happiness as a measure implies, at least indirectly, a critique of the way we have looked upon societal development until now. Historically, we have measured progress in societies by using monetary metrics – Gross National Product per capita, in particular, is often used as a core metric for the welfare and well-being of societies. This is questioned in Chapter 5 with a discussion of new ways of measuring progress; and the chapter also includes presentation of new societal indexes trying to capture monetary as well as non-monetary aspects of societal development.

Finally, Chapter 6 concludes and sums up the presentation and why it is important to think about welfare in the years to come. The chapter will also present some key issues to be aware of – especially for the welfare states in their search for happy populations, and how social policy can play a role in relation to happy societies.

2

WHAT IS HAPPINESS?

INTRODUCTION

This chapter will outline the relation between central social science disciplines and happiness, but will also show how this cuts across the disciplines and thus increases our understanding of individual people's behaviour. Classical economics, for example, uses the individual utility-maximising as the basis for understanding how societies function. However, this is typically measured by an assumption that our behaviour is strongly, or almost exclusively, influenced by monetary issues, neglecting more intrinsic aspects related to well-being. For example, we might work not only for financial reward, but also to carry out a job with meaning and the ability to be fulfilling and increase our well-being. In addition, the chapter aims to present a variety of understandings of happiness. Is it a feeling; is it well-being; or do we have to be more specific based upon how we have seen life develop? Can we be sure that individuals can distinguish between a moment of happiness and the lasting feeling of happiness?

A starting point for an analysis of the concept is to look into its linguistic origins. In Middle English, *hap* refers to chance, fortune or luck, which then also leads to including "pleasurable feeling that results from attaining success or good fortune" (Duncan, 2005: 21). Thus, this is clearly a focus resulting from having both a good life and success and, in this way, the semantic understanding is in line with the more philosophical approaches.

Philosophers have had ideas about what happiness is and these will be used as starting points for a presentation of what happiness is, and how we can understand happiness in the present day (cf. also Diener and Seligman, 2004; Haidt *et al.*, 2008, Schumaker, 2007; Smith, 2008). Happiness is often used interchangeably with words like satisfaction, utility, well-being and so on (Easterlin, 2001). Often, this has been done without acknowledging the fact that they have been defined differently or have had different connotations or understandings throughout the history of mankind. A starting point for the departure is the Aristotelian view that happiness can be defined. See also later in the chapter, as related to at least some of the following elements: prosperity, an independent life, and the ability to enjoy pleasure. This is further related to whether happiness and the good society are interlinked.

Therefore, utilitarian philosophy is, for example, being interested in how public policy should aim at greater happiness for a greater number of people. If this is the goal then it is important to understand not only the concept, but also what will influence and have an impact on the level of happiness. How this then can be integrated in decision making is the focus of Chapter 4. Furthermore, we will discuss whether the goal of happiness should be included in policy making, and how the relationship between the welfare state and happiness can be understood. Will some areas then be more important to policy makers than they are today? Will including happiness change the calculations of what are the most important decisions to take in societies? And might they also contradict more classical positions, such as cost–benefit analysis, if they have to include well-being in the calculations?

Sometimes well-being, utility and happiness are used interchangeably, and therefore the use and understanding of these concepts are also important. One definition of well-being is "a life that matches an individual's own ideals. We think of income, affect, and well-being judgments as alternative indicators of well-being" (Diener *et al.*, 2009: 20). This also indicates a core issue that discussion of, and aspects related to, happiness will have to include – the individual subjective evaluation of life and conditions related to life. However, in the presentation below, and as a recurrent theme across the book, we will consider whether the relationship between micro- and macro-level is possible to establish and use as a guideline, without the causal relation always needing to be clear.

THE GOOD SOCIETY AND HAPPINESS

Happiness is a part of the good society and the good life, and utopian communities are often described as happy societies. But what is happiness? Can we, at a societal level, understand happiness when it relates to the individual's experiences, and when it appears to be associated with the left-hand part of the brain and not the right? These are the two key questions that this chapter will discuss. However, the chapter will also discuss happiness and welfare in light of how we can understand and evaluate what welfare is, and whether there is a relationship between happiness and prosperity, although it might be pointed out early on that the "distinction between them may for all purposes of action be neglected" (Pollock, 1877: 270).

Happiness is a basic sense of satisfaction (Layard, 2005) and, vice versa, a situation marked by discouragement and discontent could not be characterised as happy. That does not mean that we need constantly and always to find ourselves in a situation where we are happy. Life has its ups and downs. Therefore, there will be times when some people are happy, others unhappy, and this also helps to explain why happiness might vary over the life cycle (Clark and Oswald, 2002; Clark, 2007; Blanchflower and Oswald, 2008; Fischer, 2009). Furthermore, the analysis will delve also into why happiness can vary over time.

Happiness can be understood theoretically in many ways, and philosophers have been preoccupied with this through the ages. The question is also whether, and if so how, happiness and unhappiness can be measured at the same time and combined into an overall expression of the whole society's average happiness.

Still, the ambition of the good society is seemingly to enhance most people's welfare. This will also include the possibility that they can be happy at least part of the time. Maximising the amount of time individuals can be happy might thus be a new goal for the good society. If this goal is important, then it is even more important to understand what happiness is.

WHAT IS HAPPINESS?

Happiness has been a central goal in many communities. Historically, happiness has in many and varied ways been involved in philosophical, economic, psychological and sociological analysis (Haidt, 2006). The hunt for a recipe for a happy society, or the good society, has drawn people throughout history, and if it is not about being happy on earth, then in the after-life (Veenhoven, 2010). Veenhoven, in the early research, defined happiness as "the degree to which an individual judges the overall quality of his life favourably" (Veenhoven, 1991: 2). This understanding, to a large degree, is the one used when doing empirical research in the area. However, the question is still whether it has ever been possible to define what happiness is. Moreover, one can ask whether there is a context-independent definition of it, and how context – for example the weather – has an affect on the assessment of levels of happiness (cf. also Chapter 3) and the concrete aspect of measuring it. Diener and colleagues have focused on life-satisfaction and a joyful life, and given more limited weight to experience aspects such as anxiety and sadness (Diener *et al.*, 1997).

Happiness has been used synonymously with terms such as "subjective well-being, satisfaction, utility, well-being, and welfare" (Easterlin, 2001). Others consider that the correct word is well-being, but that use of the word "happiness" in a direct question makes it easier for the individual to understand the subject of enquiry than if the question relates to their well-being. I will use the words utility, satisfaction and well-being synonymously with happiness, but understand welfare as a broader concept. The welfare concept includes, for example, an understanding of happiness (Greve, 2008b). Happiness and its quality is thus a part of societal welfare, but other aspects such as economic opportunities are also included herein as disposable income makes it possible to achieve different consumption opportunities and levels.

Happiness could also be looked upon from the perspective of the individual or lay person. Here it seems that the central factors are (McMahan and Estes, 2010):

1. The experience of pleasure;
2. The avoidance of negative experience;
3. Self-development;
4. Contribution to others.

Still, happiness can also be understood as having a forward-looking perspective (called prospective happiness); a happiness in process; and a backward-looking perspective (called retrospective happiness) (Ho, 2010). This might have implications especially for formulating a public policy, but also how to measure happiness, as will be discussed in Chapter 3. For example, the ability to be backward looking can help in explaining the relationship between happiness and age. This has even been described as the 3P Model (Durayappah, 2010). The model, it is argued, combines top-down as well as bottom-up factors, and in relation to happiness this relates to "how happy I was, how happy I am, how happy I am going to be" (Durayappah, 2010: 5). In relation to psychology this is also presented with reference to Csikszenmihalyi's understanding of flow, for example being lost in the present without worrying about the future. The ability to look at the past, at the present and into the future is important because the understanding of the individual helps in explaining why it is methodologically possible to measure happiness.

The following analysis, from various perspectives, will focus on different understandings of happiness and how these might or can interact with each other.

Philosophy and happiness

The search for happiness through the good life has occupied philosophers for many centuries. Still today it can be seen as central that "the good life is identical with the happy life" (Brülde and Bykvist, 2010). The Greek philosopher Aritippus, in the fourth century BC, said that the goal in life was to maximise your total comfort. Another Greek philosopher, Epicurus, argued that it was a fundamental obligation to maximise pleasure and minimise pain. Plato considered that there was a duty to achieve the good life through attainment of knowledge (McMahan and Estes, 2010).

Philosophers have thus presented a series of definitions of happiness. The Greek philosopher Aristotle defined happiness as follows:

> We may define happiness as prosperity combined with excellence, or as independence of life, or as the secure enjoyment of the maximum of pleasure, or as a good condition of property and body, together with the power of guarding one's property and body and making use of them. That happiness is one or more of these things, pretty well everyone agrees.
>
> (Aristotle, quoted in Helliwell, 2003)

The focus in this definition is the combination of material wealth, security and independence with good health. It is also a very broad definition that implicitly suggests that material goods are the means to achieve happiness and not the ultimate goal in itself. "The happy man is he who lives well and acts well" (Aristotle, 2000). The acts might, albeit implicitly, also be interpreted as altruistic acts that can contribute to happiness. Other interpretations of Aristotle emphasise blessing or stability to be involved in the understanding of happiness, especially also to be sure that a sudden accident does not affect the long-term perception of happiness. For example, while there is some evidence to suggest that luck, albeit briefly, may affect one's happiness there is no clear and systematic knowledge that the level of happiness will always return to the previous level. Winning a lottery does not necessarily imply long-term improvement in one's happiness. The interaction between tangible and intangible assets is furthermore important for the good life, which therefore must be included in the measurement of welfare and prosperity (see also Chapter 5).

Aristotle also focused on what has been described as *eudaimonia* as an objective good (Lelkes, 2006). *Eudaimonia* as a good is focused mainly on the process leading toward a more psychologically satisfied level for the individual (Konow and Earley, 2008). Herodotus saw *eudaimonia* as the best position, and Thomas Aquinas emphasised the relationship of faith and happiness as well as luck. Thus, it was also the case that "happiness became thus a concept attainable for all that could be reached in the here and now. The fact we can be happy. .. Turned into a happiness value of society and laid the basis for our modern welfare state" (Schimmel,

2007: 97). *Eudaimonia* is the human desire for individual fulfilment, which includes (cf. also the understanding of subjective well-being) elements such as self-actualisation and self-realisation. *Eudaimonia* is thus one central philosophical approach to happiness focusing on how to achieve what is attainable when using the individual's abilities. However, this is not necessarily important for the individual alone but for society as a whole as human capital often is the most central resource for a society.

Another approach has focused on hedonism, on the concept that well-being consists of happiness and pleasure, where happiness has both a cognitive element focusing on life-satisfaction and an affective element with a positive mood or a combination (MacMahan and Estes, 2010). Still, another way of looking at this is that "men at most times will choose a very hard, poor, and joyless life – in short, unhappiness – rather than no life at all" (Pollock, 1877: 270). Still, the human desire for happiness, of which hedonism also is an expression, is important in the understanding of why research into happiness can inform us on the path to the good society seen from both the individual and societal level.

A core ethical question, also important when discussing utility (cf. "Happiness in economic theory", Chapter 2), is how to reconcile one person's happiness with another person's unhappiness – for example how to make a trade-off between different persons' happiness – but also other goals of societal policy (Brülde and Bykvist, 2010). This question cannot easily be answered as it involves interpersonal comparisons, but usually (cf. Chapter 3) it is done by aggregating individual preferences.

In this book, interpersonal comparison will not be in focus, despite the fact that happiness and the measurement thereof have been a way of coping with the problem of comparison of utility in economic theory, as this measure fully relies upon subjective understanding and the measurement does not try to engage in a comparison of individuals' choices of their lifestyles. Nevertheless, empirical data will provide information on differences in happiness across different groups.

Happiness in economic theory

Economists and economic theory, especially from Bentham and Mill onwards, used utility as an expression of the degree of happiness. This can be seen by the following slogan, which has been attributed to Bentham: "the greatest happiness to the greatest number is the measure of right and wrong" (Brülde and Bykvist, 2010: 3). Brülde and Bykvist, on the same page, quote Mill: "Actions are right in proportion as they tend to promote happiness, wrong as they tend to produce the reverse of happiness" (Mill, 1871: 55 cited in Brülde and Bykvist, 2010). It has even been argued that Bentham had a dream of research on happiness (Bok, 2010).

In recent years we have seen an increased interest in happiness research, and a whole subsection of economics (behavioural economics) deals intensively with aspects thereof. For an overview of behavioural economics, see Wilkinson (2008). However, the point has been also that the decisions on interventions to increase the happiness level in society should be chosen from among the sets of intervention that improve happiness most (Ng and Ho, 2006). Even if happiness can be difficult to define, utility has for a long time been seen as a way of understanding it (Pollock, 1879).

Maximising utility was seen as the way societies could achieve and have the greatest overall level of happiness. Even if the word happiness was not always used, this was the implicit meaning when discussing and analysing utility. Maximisation of society's happiness through each individual's action was thus a central axiomatic consequence of individuals' behaviour, and also a way of avoiding having to make interpersonal comparisons. Utility was seen as a collective understanding of a society's happiness or contentment, because "being happy (is) equivalent to living well and acting well" (Little, 2002: 39). The relationship between the individual person's subjective experience and the need for collectivistic intervention is often unclear in these types of approaches, and utilitarianism does not consider the distributional impact of maximising utility.

A core problem for economists was that the utility could not be measured simply and clearly (Anand and Clark, 2006). Furthermore, it was difficult to be sure that actual decisions always clearly expressed the preferences of the individual, as some often take the default position (for example the one put forward as the position to have without making an actual decision) and for others complexities in the market and limited personal experiences make it difficult to decide fully in line with the individual's preferences (Beshears *et al.*, 2008; Greve, 2009). At the same time, it has been difficult not only to measure happiness, but also to weigh the viewpoints of individuals or to put the usefulness of different people together (Peiro, 2006). The difficulty in using utility as a concept for a group of persons was already identified by

Robbins in 1932 (Frey and Stutzer, 2002b). Hence economic analysis was for many years focused on an implicit way to determine utility, and that is understood as the sum of society's activities, especially as measured by GDP (cf. also Chapter 5), for example, the actual preferences revealed by actual behaviour.

This is despite the fact that there is also made here, although mainly implicitly, a weighting of numerous individual choices and actions. But these acts are seen as that which best expresses the individual's personal preferences, and if we therefore buy more of one product than another, then in the classical sense it will mean a higher overall utility. A higher overall utility is seen as greater happiness for the whole community.

This implicit method to quantify the value of utility is therefore usually done through an indirect measurement. The emphasis is that individuals through their actions just act in a way that would maximise their utility and therefore also that of society. The acts of individuals made through the purchase of goods and services in the market have been seen as an indication of the usefulness of the various products and services, and a reflection of how individuals, including the entire society, optimise their utility. In other words, social functioning was taken as an expression of utility, and hence implicitly that the value of a country's total production was indicative of the highest utility. One problem with this, besides the difficulties in calculating GDP, is that it provides no opportunity to reveal preferences for public services; and thus leaves a problem with the assessment of how the global community can achieve the highest possible success for all citizens, even those who do not have money to buy on the market. Another problem is that the utility of goods and services is dependent not only on the outcome of the choice, but also on the context within which the choice has been made (Köszedi, 2008).

Economists have acknowledged that, supposedly, there was a decreasing advantage of rising incomes, particularly because of diminishing marginal utility. For example, the first beer or the first glass of wine tastes good, but not the tenth. This also implicitly shows that relative income is important. Expressed differently, once the basic needs such as food and drink are met, and perhaps considerably surpassed, the utility of even more food and consumer goods is relatively small. Despite this (and cf. also the next section), higher income is often associated with a higher level of happiness. Still, as a consequence of diminishing marginal utility, the earning of income also gradually becomes less important for the individual's utility or satisfaction.

The focus on utility as expressed through actions in the market has also meant that economic studies have largely avoided dealing with happiness. It is for the first time, in the last 20 to 30 years, that economists have been increasingly focused on the analysis of how happiness, economics and community development can be combined.

There may be differences in the happiness expected from making different choices, and the actual realised utility by the choice made. This reflects that people would be happier and more satisfied with the prospect of making a specific choice than with what actually came out of their choice. It can be anything from the latest clothing purchase to visiting a restaurant, travelling or playing for the big prize. The expectation of joy from a certain action, it is often said, is the greatest (Easterlin, 2001). If expected utility is larger than the achieved utility, it can affect the happiness of each individual in a negative direction. This is in line with looking at experience utility, but it also indicates that, in policy making, not only experience utility but also decision utility (for example the actual decisions) should be taken into account (Loewenstein and Ubel, 2008).

Happiness, sociology and psychology

Happiness came late into the discipline of economics. Positive psychology also relatively lately became interested, and sociology, despite having a focus on individual well-being, also entered rather late into the discussion on happiness. Psychology, as with economics, has had a focus on behaviour as the only way to interpret individuals' activities (cf. research such as Pavlov and Skinner). As Layard has put it: "... behaviourism was the intellectual climate of the 1930s" (Layard, 2003: 4).

In recent years there has been an almost explosive interest in the topic from many disciplines, and examples in psychology are Snyder and Lopez. The sociologist Veenhoven has published extensively (cf. References). A clear reason for this is that important non-economic factors have an impact on happiness, such as "social capital, democratic governance, and human rights" (Diener and Seligman, 2004: 1).

In sociology the focus is on social relations and how individuals act in different situations. In this context, therefore, happiness also implies security, trust and how the individual is and lives compared to others (cf. also "Happiness and income" in the next section). Social capital, therefore, also has a central role in the analysis of happiness (Kroll, 2008) – and this relates to aspects such as trust as mentioned above – but also obligations, norms and sanctions, looking back to one of the original understandings of social capital (Coleman, 1988), and as made popular by Putnam's book *Bowling Alone* (Field, 2008). Besides trust and norms, others point to how information channels are important in relation to social capital. Information channels are understood as social relations through contacts with family and friends (cf. also data for this in Chapter 3). Individual factors thereby also have an impact on happiness. These focus on elements such as optimism, self-esteem, personal control and extroversion (Leung *et al.*, 2010). Leung and colleagues also point to the fact that neuroticism has a negative impact on happiness. Social capital is an important part of societal development (Oorschot and Arts, 2005) and thereby also, given what has been mentioned above, it is an important aspect of happiness and a happy society. This further might be part of the explanation why voluntary work can be of importance for the well-being of society and presumably not especially due to the work being done, but more due to what the individual himself or herself gains from the activity.

Lack of norms and rules for behaviour, in an understanding borrowed from Durkheim, might help to explain why at the same time as we have become richer, well-being or happiness has remained constant and the depression rates have increased (Haidt *et al.*, 2008).

Positive psychology has its focus on the subjective level, on positive subjective experience in various phases over the life cycle. This includes well-being and satisfaction (seen as past elements) and happiness as the present elements, whereas the future is related to optimism and hope (Seligman, 2002b).

In the psychological approach to happiness this has further focused on central aspects such as intrinsic motivation and also elements from Maslow's hierarchy of needs. Furthermore, adaptation level theory and social comparison theory are inspired by psychology (Easterlin, 2001). A distinction between intrinsic and extrinsic factors can thus be important but also, as will be referred to several times, adaptation to a level can have an impact. For example, despite our differences we can quickly become used to a certain living standard.

The focus has often been on the level of the individual's concerns rather than broadly on their life satisfaction. Therefore the ability to reach a certain level of life satisfaction is important. Education can thus be important, for example, due to the fact that training provides opportunities in the sense used by Nobel laureate Amartya Sen of the importance of what we can do, since Sen's focus has been on the capabilities and the room for opportunities this creates. The opportunities created by individual skills can be seen as a social framework, thus giving the individual a set of options that can be selected from the person's individual preferences. As Sen (2008: 24) puts it: "The capability of a person reflects the alternative combinations of functioning the person can attain, and from which he or she can choose one collection."

Capabilities can be called well-being freedom (Lelkes, 2006a: 287). The important aspect of it is that capability can be understood as what people actually can do and what they have the option to do, given that how to use personal abilities is dependent on the institutional set-up (Goerne, 2010).

The most difficult problem in an approach based on options is that it has been difficult to operationalise and measure what is meant by capability. But while it is intuitively clear that having capabilities also offers greater chances to live a happy life, it is less clear what society's role can be in that respect. How the environment can be designed for individuals while taking into account how the public interest can be preserved is thus a key element of a happy society. It is therefore also a given that access to and use of social indicators and the measurement of happiness could be a possibility, albeit still only partially an approach to compensate for the difficulties of operationalising a set of possibilities in Sen's understanding. Sen also pointed out that the focus on utility and success

> can be deeply unfair to those who are persistently deprived, such as the traditional underdogs in stratified societies, oppressed minorities in intolerant communities, precarious sharecroppers living in a world of uncertainty, sweated workers in exploitative industrial arrangements, subdued housewives in deeply sexist cultures.
>
> (Sen, 2009: 18)

Nonetheless, Sen believes that "happiness is not all that matters, but first of all, it does matter" (2009: 27).

The sociological and psychological approach is thus to a high degree pointing not only to the opportunities, but also to the interaction and relation between people. This also emphasises that when trying to analyse and understand happiness, one needs to look into everyday life, and individual persons' relations to each other. Being together, having social capital (Field, 2008) and being integrated into society therefore have an important function.

In the vein of these approaches, happiness can also be understood as the absence of negative aspects such as anxiety, depression and insecurity, or at least other important elements in the understanding of a happy life (Argyle, 2001). As Myers has argued, happiness is about "a high ratio of positive to negative feelings" (Myers, 2004: 522). It might even be, as in the so-called hive hypothesis, that it can be argued that people need to "lose themselves occasionally by becoming part of an emergent social organism in order to reach the highest level of human flourishing" (Haidt *et al.*, 2008: 133).

Still, there is also the risk that it is a false promise as expressed in the following way: "The second smart lie is that we are free to choose, because we are rational autonomous beings and, as such, can even choose to change ourselves" (Veenhoven, 2008a: 385).

From this can be deduced that relations are important, but also that aspiration and adaptation is central in order to grasp the understanding and varieties of happiness.

Happiness and income

It is difficult to argue that happiness should be an absolute phenomenon. Conversely, happiness is considered to be relative (Oswald, 1997). One consequence is that happiness may depend on how it compares with other people in other countries, etc. Another consequence of fortune relativity applies to the hedonic treadmill, or the Easterlin Paradox, describing how we do not necessarily become happier by having a higher income (Konow and Earley, 2008). Easterlin has described it in the following way:

> Income growth does not, however, cause well-being to rise, either for higher or lower income persons, because it generates equivalent growth in material aspirations, and the negative effect of the latter on subjective well-being undercuts the positive effect of the former.
>
> (Easterlin, 2001: 481)

We will return to the explanations and implications of this in a wide variety of contexts throughout this book. The discussion can also be related to the fact that relative income is part of the more general aspiration-level theory, and by this going back to Veblen's "conspicuous consumption" (Frey and Stutzer, 2002a: 411) and also Dusenberry's theory of relative income and Hirsch's positional goods. Dusenberry's theory has also been seen as a component of how rising aspirations have an impact, and this can then also be used to explain variations in happiness (Graham, 2009).

There are basically two schools of thought and approaches to explain the link between income and the degree of our happiness.

One is represented by Easterlin, who suggests that happiness depends on the individual's relative position and income. Later, however, he increasingly focused on aspiration as a key explanatory element of the correlation between income and happiness. Income may not only be involved as a simple variable to understand happiness, but it may be introduced and considered in conjunction with the context in which income can be used. In other words, if we fail to meet our expectations this will affect our happiness. Income thus has a large impact on the level of happiness. Furthermore, even if those with higher incomes are generally happier than others, raising income does not necessarily raise the happiness of all. The main reason for this is that the norms on how to judge happiness also change (Easterlin, 1995).

The second school also draws on the concept of relative income. Sociologist Ruut Veenhoven, for instance, has argued that the relative level only has a meaning after a certain base level is reached, i.e. that "the wealth to low levels of income helps satisfy basic needs and increases SWB [social well-being], but after needs are satisfied additional income has little or no effect on happiness" (Konow and Earley, 2008: 4). Veenhoven's formulation is indirectly a reformulation of Allard's theories about "having, loving and being" and, consequently, that it is important to look at various social indicators, as money alone cannot explain the degree of happiness either for the individual or for society as a whole.

However, in his early work, Veenhoven rejected the idea that happiness could be relative, but instead he argued for a focus on "innate bio-psychological needs which do not adjust to circumstances: needs mark in fact the limits of human adaptability" (Veenhoven, 1991: 32). Using the relative level might also help us to understand why sometimes poor people are happier than rich people.

A separate issue is with whom to compare oneself. Who is the point of reference, is it the neighbour, the most affluent or successful, or those often in the media? The point of reference thus has an impact on the degree of happiness, and can also have an impact on why older people, despite reduced health and mobility, might still find that they have lived a happy life – and are happier than younger people who at that point of time perhaps have a higher income and appear more successful. Even more, this might also be part of the explanation why in the US "the black–white difference is much larger than the gender difference" (Yang, 2008: 207).

Although there is general support for the relative point of view, the results of surveys of happiness are not entirely in agreement. In their study, Diener and colleagues found:

> The present results do not give support to a relative standard approach, they also do not completely uphold a simple universal needs approach. Income seems to have some effect on happiness far beyond the level of meeting subsistence needs. There is some support, however, for the idea that finances have less and less effect as one ascends the income ladder.
>
> (Diener *et al.*, 1993: 220)

There is also an indication that "people rank happiness and satisfaction ahead of money as a life goal" (Diener and Seligman, 2004: 2). One reason for an increase in happiness besides the impact of the relative position can be that "happiness is positively correlated with income but negatively correlated with unrealized aspirations" (Okulicz-Kozaryn, 2010: 227). Or it might be that it is not the actual development in the growth in income (or GDP), but rather the change and acceleration that has an impact, and this can be explained by the fact that the individual has more than his/her expectations fulfilled (Bjørnskov *et al.*, 2007b).

Another study indicates that looking into the development over time in 52 countries, happiness in fact rose in 45 of them. This might also seem to imply that initially economic gains have an impact on happiness, however, after having reached a certain level the lifestyle, including elements of social tolerance and democracy, become still more important (Inglehart *et al.*, 2008).

Even though there is disagreement on the Easterlin Paradox, it helps to underline and "expos[e] the deep complexities of the determinants of human welfare and the limits to which those determinants can be captured simply via a specification of the income variable" (Graham, 2009: 45).

Some of the consequences of the positions above, as will be elaborated in the discussion on the use of GDP as a yardstick (cf. Chapter 5), and on labour market policy and jobs (cf. Chapter 4), are that changes in income are more important than the actual level. It also shows that the use of economic theory alone will give only a limited assessment of how and why a society and individuals are happy.

HAPPINESS AND WELFARE

Happiness and welfare – are they connected? This is a central question given that most (western societies, at least) prefer to describe themselves as welfare states. Therefore, knowledge of what welfare is and the possible link between the two elements is important. First, we will discuss what welfare is.

Welfare can be described as having sufficient economic wealth, which makes it possible to buy a wide range of goods and services. Welfare in this understanding is mainly an economic approach, based on the idea that what individuals benefit from a good or service is crucial to an understanding of what welfare is (van Praag, 1993). In economic theory it is the concept of utility and how to maximise individuals' and society's total utility, which is therefore central (cf. also "What is happiness?", p. 17). A person's utility of a product or service need not be the same as other people's. Utility is thus difficult to quantify for a community. Welfare is, therefore, in this approach, empirically measured by looking at the value of a society's total output measured as annual GDP (gross domestic product) per capita. The development in GDP is therefore also a metric for the analysis, including the discussion on the Easterlin Paradox, of how happiness develops when increases or decreases in GDP take place. This is not, as we will see in Chapter 5, an acceptance that GDP alone is a good measure for the welfare in a society.

The welfarist approach and tradition seemingly indicates that well-being is derived from the consumption of goods and services (Slesnick, 1998). Another way to describe this is to look into more ethical aspects also – "Welfarism is the view that nothing but welfare matters" (Sumner, 2003: 184) – but also that in relation to ethical issues it is a normative theory related to morality.

Welfare and utility need not be the same for everyone. The individual may have different needs and different preferences when it comes to a choice between alternative goods and experiences. Welfare might be more free time for some, while for others it can be an exciting job and more work. The same relates to happiness. Happiness for one can almost be misfortune for someone else. Recognising these different needs and perceptions of what makes us happy helps to explain why it is so difficult to move from what the individual prefers that society must do to a consensus that this is the right decision. The balance between community and individual aspirations and responsibilities and who best solves the conflicts is not clear or simple to make. A society might take a decision that improves some person's happiness, but is contrary to other individuals' wishes and thus may affect their happiness. This cannot be decided beforehand on a theoretical analysis, which implies a need for solid empirical analysis involving quantitative as well as qualitative analysis.

Still, we know as individuals, or have at least a fairly clear view upon, how different aspects can have an impact on, for example, our well-being when we decided whom to marry, where to work, etc. Thus, welfare is also a central issue of "our common-sense morality" (Sumner, 2003: 2).

Welfare can be defined and measured by objective or subjective approaches. Objective welfare is about material resources and objective aspects in relation to the quality of life, whereas subjective well-being includes subjective evaluation of the experience of satisfaction/dissatisfaction with the material conditions of life or social relations with other people (Allardt, 2003).

One could argue that eight dimensions should be included (Stiglitz *et al.*, 2009: 14–15):

1. Material living standards;
2. Health;
3. Education;
4. Personal activities including work;

5. Political voice and governance;
6. Social connections and relationships;
7. Environment;
8. Insecurity, of an economic as well as physical nature.

These elements will, to a large degree, be those that will be examined further in Chapter 4, as they also resemble many of the issues that arise when analysing what can have an impact on happiness. The central exceptions are environment and education. Education has already been touched upon, because we know education has an impact on several of the other elements among the eight points. They resemble the OECD's social indicators (OECD, 2006), which also include more elements in relation to money (although that is included in point 1 above) and then try to measure well-being across a number of indicators and included in this is the calculation of a composite indicator. Still, "'no man is an island, entire of itself; every man is a piece of the continent': people's happiness depends to a large extent on the circumstances of the broader community they are part of and their relationship to it" (OECD, 2006: 12, quoting the poet John Donne).

Welfare can also be seen as a relative term. This means that prosperity, and especially the individual's perception of welfare, may depend on other people's welfare more than the actual level. It is often called the neighbour effect, meaning that one person's welfare is measured against whether one's neighbour has the same goods and services as oneself. A good can thus have "higher" value if the neighbour does not have the good than if the neighbour does. This also explains why for some having the newest gadgets, for example, is important as a kind of status symbol. Welfare is thus more than the direct economic benefit of various goods and services.

In sociological theory, an understanding of welfare is that the most "basic form of welfare is well-being" (Walker, 1997: 212). By putting emphasis on well-being, a wider group of elements such as a good environment, good health, peace of mind in everyday life, etc., will be included.

Welfare is thus not a unique concept – it will presumably involve elements that are both about a society's overall wealth and opportunity to distribute a range of goods and services, but also about how and what each person has and what opportunities individuals have the capability to unfold.

It can thus clearly be assumed that welfare is influenced by elements at both societal and individual level. The key elements are (Greve, 2008):

Society level: GDP per capita and expenditure on welfare policies

Individual level: Happiness and the number of persons living in poverty

At the community level, the level of GDP per capita is assumed to have an impact on welfare, but presumably also on happiness, because a higher level of income may have an impact on their happiness. Recall the Easterlin Paradox, however, and the possibility that more welfare spending may lead to more welfare for the individual. At the individual level the focus is on the subjective perception of happiness because it encapsulates a large number of individual factors on the individual's welfare level. The number of people living in poverty describes the degree of inequality that may have an impact on welfare in a society. This also implies that happiness has an impact on welfare for individuals as well as societies. Naturally, several other elements could be included (cf. also Chapter 5 for new measures and other elements to be included herein).

A reason for including and looking into comparison is also, besides the neighbour effect as mentioned above, that one needs to be able to analyse whether, for example, if we increase the welfare "of a rich person by $1000 and lower the welfare of a poor person by $500, has social welfare increased or decreased?"(Slesnick, 1998: 2140).

There may be a correlation between happiness and welfare, or there may not. Which way the relationship goes is not completely clear, although there is every indication that more and more welfare increases happiness. This will also be shown in later chapters. However, the analysis also shows that the focus on the quality of life, and not measured exclusively in economic terms, is central for the under-standing of societal as well as individual life conditions. Also related to this is, therefore, whether more is always better (Mau and Verwiebe, 2010).

SUMMING UP

Happiness can thus be understood as a broad term that is individually experienced and is well founded, but which, through analysis and data collection, it is indeed possible to measure and achieve a clear understanding of even at the community level. Happiness is thus defined as individuals' perception of their lives in the past and the present and their expectations for the future.

It is thus possible also to compare countries and development-ments over time. The level of consistency and the ability to connect happiness with individual factors such as education and marriage should not be overestimated, although the connection is important. The question is also whether there is a correlation between happiness and prosperity, and then if this is a stable relation.

Happiness is a comprehensive concept that largely looks at and is evaluated by the individual's perceptions. It has also meant that measurements of happiness have not been particularly widespread. However, in recent years there has been a growing use of indicators on happiness (cf. also Chapter 3).

Can happiness be put into a formula? Hardly, but it has been tried. A happiness formula is described by a correlation between the circumstances of life, factors which the individual can control and a set of options (Seligman, 2002a). Seligman suggests that there is a difference between a moment of happiness (for example, by a lottery win) and more lasting happiness. A happiness formula will not be part of the analysis here. This is due to the fact that the focus is at community level, and also on how to identify the factors that can affect happiness. The attempt is not to have one recipe for happi-ness, but more to be able to understand important aspects and elements influencing the happiness of individuals and societies. Still, happiness varies over life, and a moment of happiness can be important for the lifelong understanding thereof.

3

CAN WE MEASURE HAPPINESS?

INTRODUCTION

This chapter will take a methodological point of view to discuss whether it is meaningful and possible to analyse and measure happiness. This is related to the way questions are asked, the context in which they are asked, and also that there might be differences between individuals as to how they perceive happiness and what has an impact on happiness. Still, analysis and data collection have been attempted. That has shown that the answer to the questions on happiness relates to changes in the brain, and in this way the data do seem to indicate that at the least when asking a representative number of people it is possible to measure their understanding of happiness, and also how this can be related to other interpretations of societal development. In addition, the chapter presents a series of data on happiness and its relation to central parameters in Europe and the USA.

A number of studies on what affects well-being indicate that 80 per cent of the differences in happiness between nations and individuals can be explained by six factors: divorce, unemployment, trust, membership of religious organisations, faith in God, and the quality of government. In addition, there is a link between the degree of happiness and the degree of equality (Layard, 2005). Divorce is negatively correlated to happiness, whereas marriage, education level, good health and religion are positively related with happiness (Argyle, 1999; Clark and Oswald, 2002; Diener *et al.*, 1999; Frey and Stutzer, 2002a). Another analysis shows that there is evidence of a correlation between usefulness, happiness and the good life, since there is "evidence of links between life satisfaction and income, labor market participation, health, housing and social relationship" (Anand and Clark, 2006). Health also has an impact (Lelkes, 2006a). Elements such as work and labour market participation, health, voluntary activities and social cohesion are thus key elements, while there is also a focus on how and whether a society can help to create greater happiness (cf. also Chapter 4). The main part of these elements was already pointed to by Wilson in 1967, who argued that happiness was related to "young, healthy, well-educated, well-paid, extroverted, optimistic, worry-free, religious and married persons with high self-esteem, job morale, modest aspiration, of either sex and a wide range of intelligence" (Wilson, 1967, here from Helliwell, 2003: 333).

When analysing across countries, what affects happiness in one country need not necessarily be related to the factors that may have an effect in another country. An analysis suggests, for example, that the economic climate, the end of communism, the number of chambers in parliament, political stability and child mortality have an impact on the degree of satisfaction. Surveys have also shown, as indicated above, that family life is important.

Whether or not it can be inferred from the surveys with sufficient precision that family life is the greatest contribution to greater happiness, across 44 countries married people live on average three years longer than unmarried and have better physical and mental health than unmarried people. Here the focus will mainly be on the direction and consistency more than the actual size of the direction, since there is a large uncertainty to this. Correlation, in other words, is an indicator with which to take stock of the situation, a kind of compass, without it being capable of describing the speed or the means of transport to move from one situation to a better situation. Furthermore, it is not certain that all persons needing to move in the same direction as the individual can have and do have different preferences, even though society as an average might become happier by moving in a certain direction. The discussion on relative impact, and whether initiatives can be taken only if they fulfil the classical Pareto-criteria, is not included in the analysis.

It is certain that happiness can be found at various levels and has different relations and impact. Three different levels can be discerned (Nettle, 2005: 18):

1. Instant happiness.
2. Assessment of happiness (satisfaction, well-being).
3. Quality of life (achievement of life goals, meeting expenses etc.).

This classification may help to explain the happiness of someone who experiences fleeting change in well-being in the first level. It may, for example, have been only a brief moment of happiness, which was obtained by finding a €500 banknote on the road or by a lottery win. Whether by this example one can conclude that it would be good for society to have more such winners is another issue. The second level is more heartfelt and based on an overall assessment of the situation, whereas the third level is something more deeply rooted.

In the third level, the individual's aspirations and desires are substantially met. What level the individual is on, when asked about their happiness, thus affects the answer, but this may also apply to a wide range of other studies. At the same time, a series of moments of immediate success will presumably contribute to a more positive assessment of the overall level of happiness.

Questions related to adaptation and its impact on happiness will also be included in the presentation.

The focus will be especially on the USA, and on Europe as an entity. For Europe, the European Social Survey will mainly be used to present data on happiness and its development, and reference will also be made to the world value survey. For the USA, the main database used has been the General Social Survey, as this also includes data on happiness although on a less detailed scale (very happy, pretty happy and not too happy), compared with the scale for the European survey (in the next section). For information on the European Social Survey, see Appendix at end of this chapter. Data and the relation to social issues are chosen based upon the knowledge of where there might be an impact, and at the same time an influence, on individuals' lives.

CAN WE MEASURE HAPPINESS?

Central, of course, is the question of whether it is possible to measure happiness. Is it possible to find out whether you and I are happy, and if it is only our own subjective assessment that counts, is it necessarily an expression of truth?

One problem with polls, and also surveys such as those used in happiness research, is that statements may be influenced by contextual factors such as whether the sun is shining the day we are asked, or we have just won €100. The question is, therefore, whether it is possible to measure happiness and what we can interpret from these answers. Clearly the measurement is an approach where one is relying on the expressed preferences rather than the preferences revealed by actual behaviour (Graham, 2009). This also highlights the necessity to be aware that even actual behaviour, for example when shopping, might be manipulated and, therefore, even if it does reveal preferences this might also later be understood or reduced to a negative feeling given that the money is now spent and perhaps it would actually have been better to pay a bill.

Most measurements of happiness are based on simply asking each person how he or she feels about happiness. It is done by asking questions about how people have it when all things are taken into account. On a worldwide basis, it is possible to gain information through the World Values Survey (http://www.worldvaluessurvey.org/), just as there is a website with information about happiness in the world. The European value studies in the European Social Survey are also useful to assess progress in happiness, both in individual years as over time, and in European countries overall and in individual countries. Currently, there are studies available from 2002, 2004, 2006 and 2008. In particular, data from the European Social Survey will be used to illustrate relations between happiness and different aspects of life based upon averages for all Europeans participating in the studies, so the analysis will provide only a more limited look into differences between countries. In the USA, the General Social Survey has for many years measured the level of happiness, which also helps to explain why it is possible to analyse and discuss the Easterlin Paradox, for example. There is even in the USA cumulative knowledge based upon the time period 1972–2006.

Measuring happiness is typically based on the question: How happy are you? This is measured on a scale of 0–10, where 0 is extremely unhappy and 10 is extremely happy. The following scale is displayed to those participating in the European survey:

CARD 18

Extremely unhappy   Extremely happy

0   1   2   3   4   5   6   7   8   9   10

However, can one measure happiness, as described above, by getting people to rank the degree of how happy they are? This approach has drawn many criticisms pointing at different aspects.

The first problem is whether it is possible to judge how happy you are using a scale. Can an individual rank his/her degree of happiness? Studies suggest that there actually is a relationship between the answers respondents give when at the same time the researchers observe how happy they are. Thus it is possible to use this type of study and questions to compare and aggregate individual persons' happiness (Frey and Stutzer, 2002a). At the same time, it is not difficult to ask for people's subjective perception of their level of satisfaction, happiness or position on other issues. There will always be some uncertainty associated with making this kind of analysis relying on individuals' subjective viewpoints, but this does not change the general picture of those studies and surveys providing an assessment of how the individual feels. The validity of most studies of satisfaction and happiness is therefore generally high (Hoorn, 2008).

Weighting is another problem. It is debatable whether it is possible, especially in comparisons between countries, but it is a minor problem when using the same method to compare across countries. Furthermore, it can be debated whether the weighting is important given that we have the relative distance between the different answers.

A third problem may be that a question about happiness is understood differently in different countries, and that there may be specific factors that have had an impact in individual countries, such as sudden increase in income, political upheavals in the past in Eastern Europe, etc. Different cultures may not have similar perceptions of what happiness is. However, as we are looking at individuals' answers, this is a lesser problem, also due to the fact that the focus is on whether individuals are happy, more than if they are happy in the same way as others.

Overall, there is no indication that the problem is large, including that it should be methodologically more difficult to measure happiness than answers in other types of surveys and to analyse other social and societal changes.

Another methodological problem is that when people assess whether they are happy or not, this may depend on whether they have just experienced something positive or negative, or even whether the sun is shining or it has been raining that day. A study showed that if questions began with the interviewer asking about the weather, or if it was stated that it was nice weather on that day, then it could affect people's perception of whether they were happy (Nettle, 2005). This leads to an uncertainty regarding the outcome. Perhaps one should therefore also include how often they have enjoyed positive experiences and/or negative emotions (Prycker, 2010). However, it does not change that, when one is carrying out the studies under uniform conditions, they give after all a picture of what the subjective perception of happiness is.

Analyses of whether the studies show a correlation between an individual's actual opinion and their level of satisfaction show that there is likely to be a high degree of reliability, even when looking at facial expressions, measurement of activity in the brain, etc. (Kapacyr, 2008). Thus figures from a wide range of investigations may also be used to look at trends in happiness and can be used as an indicator of society's overall development in one direction or another.

This means that the numbers and metrics for success must be interpreted with caution. Still, measurements of happiness have made it possible to a greater degree than before to assess individuals' assessments of their life situations, and also eventually made measurements that together form a coherent pattern of knowledge about what affects happiness at individual and societal level.

The analysis throughout this book will look particularly critically at whether there may exist a correlation between the measurement of happiness and a number of factors. Methodologically it is difficult to establish causal relationships because happiness can be influenced by many and varied factors, especially when looking at trends over time. Particularly in relation to the measurement and evolution of happiness over time, one of the criticisms is that it is an absolute scale (Johns and Ormerod, 2007). We have, they argue, therefore reached such a high level that it will be difficult actually to achieve higher levels, since it is only getting worse and this may result in a more negative evaluation of a community's overall happiness. It is certain that the application of an absolute scale puts limits on how high an average can be, but there will be ways to tackle this problem. One way would be to attribute extra value to the fact that some are at the top, and thus it becomes a specific target that several persons obtain and/or continue to be at the highest level of happiness and therefore answer that they are extremely happy. Still, to examine the trend over time for the same individuals, and thus not only acquire data based on a particular time but also to assess trends over time for a group of people, will provide information on patterns and developments.

At the same time analysis suggests that most people, when answering the question, will give an answer which is linked not to the short term, but to their long-term assessment of how their lives are (Layard, 2005). They are thus also able to recognise that there will be ups and downs throughout life. One can therefore see the measurement of happiness as being complementary to activities, particularly in relation to an assessment of welfare in a society. It is further so that "happiness assessments are subject to vagaries and fickleness. On the other hand, so is everything interesting you want to measure" (Nettle, 2005: 68). Another way of describing this is that "happiness is just like noise. There are many qualities of noise, from a trombone to a caterwaul. But they can all be compared in terms of decibels" (Layard, 2003).

There can be many and various kinds of calculations of the correlation between happiness and social conditions and the factors which particularly affect the degree of happiness in a society. The next section will present a few empirical examples of the possible relations between core aspects of societal life and happiness, because the empirical examples are important in order to understand the relation between happiness and central welfare policy areas.

HAPPINESS: A FEW EMPIRICAL EXAMPLES

We are most happy when having sex, socialising after work, at dinner or relaxing, and less happy when commuting or working, as a study based upon 1,000 working women in Texas showed (cited in Layard, 2003). The same data information come from studies by the OECD (2009). The Texas study was based on an attempt to explain the fluctuation of the moods of individuals. The focus here will be more on the general approach to the degree of happiness, including a few aspects related to the development over time.

In this section, therefore, some data on happiness will be presented. Several examples of the relation between happiness and other factors will be shown. Further examples will be presented in Chapter 4. One aspect difficult to measure is whether it is intrinsic elements, such as relatedness and personal development, or extrinsic elements, such as wealth, personal position etc., which have a role (Ng, 2002), and furthermore the importance of the ability to reflect on past, present and future. However, using and looking at elements such as having contact with others informs us about intrinsic aspects and the types of differences this can make.

A core issue in analysis of happiness has been the relation between income and happiness. In Figure 3.1, the position with regard to income and the level of happiness is shown for selected countries.

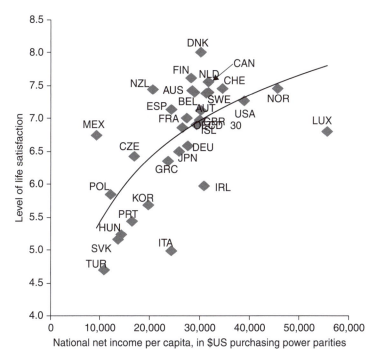

Figure 3.1 Income in selected countries and life satisfaction, 2006.
Source: OECD (2009) which has based the figure upon World Happiness Database, 2006, and GDP per capita, 2006.

Figure 3.1 is a clear indication of the relation between life satisfaction and income. In general, life satisfaction is positively related to income so that higher income implies a higher level of life satisfaction, although as always there are exceptions. Italy and Luxembourg have a lower level of happiness and Denmark a higher level than the data should indicate.

Table 3.1 shows for the EU countries (participating in the European Social Survey) the average level of happiness and its development since 2002, when the survey was started, and thereby including the four rounds so far.

Table 3.1 shows that in general the level of happiness is high in Europe and relatively stable. The slight decline can be explained by the fact that several of the new countries involved are from less affluent regions with a lower level of happiness. The World Database on Happiness shows from 1945 to 2005 a slight increase in the level of happiness despite the fact that this was also a time of increasing wealth and income. The data from the USA and Europe have been

Table 3.1 Happiness in Europe since 2002

	2002	2004	2006	2008
Average happiness	7.3	7.4	7.3	7.2

Source: European Social Survey round 1–4 (http://nesstar.ess. nsd.uib.no/webview/).
Note: The average is calculated by using 0 for extremely unhappy and 10 for extremely happy. There is a slight difference in the number of countries involved (it has been increasing to cover 31 countries in the 2008 wave).

part of the reason why it has been asserted that there is no clear relation between income and happiness. An analysis of the period from 1995 to 2007 showed, however, a relation with GDP (five years before the survey), with Latin American countries above the line and ex-communist countries below the line, and most OECD countries on the level with a stable relation between income and happiness (Inglehart *et al.*, 2008).

Table 3.2 shows the relation between happiness and subjective perception of one's own health, since studies have shown that a relation between health and happiness seems to exist.

Table 3.2 is a clear indication that at least the subjective evaluation of health has a significant impact on the level of happiness, so that those who have a subjective feeling of having a very bad level of health also have a significantly lower level of happiness. This implies, as discussed in Chapter 4, that increasing and improving the level of health can be an important aspect of how to increase a society's

Table 3.2 Happiness and subjective health evaluation, 2008

Level of subjective health evaluation	Average level of happiness
Very good	7.9
Good	7.2
Fair	6.4
Bad	5.4
Very bad	4.4
All	6.9

Source: European Social Survey, 2008 (http://nesstar.ess. nsd.uib.no/webview/) and own calculations (cf. Table 3.1).

level of happiness. Even though it is subjective, there is a clear emphasis that having good health is important. Whether this also implies a need for a policy of equality of happiness is another matter.

Figure 3.2 shows how inequality and happiness might be related. It shows a clear relation between the degree of inequality and life satisfaction, indicating that the levels of inequality have an impact on the degree of happiness in a society. The data in the figure are in line with other studies

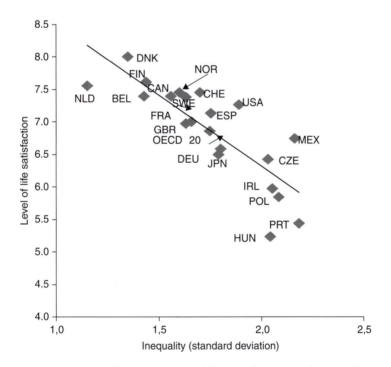

Figure 3.2 The relation between life satisfaction and inequality. *Source*: OECD, 2009.

where it has been argued that inequality has a negative impact on happiness (Schimmel, 2007). In the European Social Survey there is also a positive relation between happiness and the viewpoint that differences in living standard should be small. This is also a topic we will be returning to in Chapter 4.

Figure 3.3 shows the relation between happiness and trust in politicians in Europe. People who have trust in politicians in most cases are happier than other people. This follows the expectation that trust in others, including the political system, will increase the degree of happiness. A trusting society thus seems to be a happy society.

Trust is not only an issue in relation to the political system, but also trust for other people in general. Table 3.3 shows the relation between whether people can be trusted and the general level of happiness for the USA.

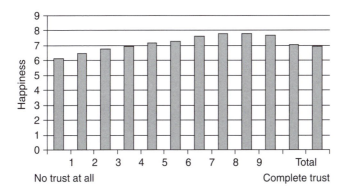

Figure 3.3 Trust in politicians and average level of happiness in 2008.
Source: Based upon European Social Survey (http://nesstar. ess.nsd.uib.no/webview/) and own calculations.

Table 3.3 The relation between trust and happiness in the US

General happiness	Trust (%)		
	Can trust	Cannot trust	Depends
Very happy	45.7	49.9	4.4
Pretty happy	38.5	56.7	4.8
Not too happy	22.5	73.4	4.1
Total	38.8	56.6	4.6

Source: General Social Surveys, 1972–2006, cumulative file.
Note: The table is based upon 31,745 answers.

Table 3.3 is also a further indication of the relation in the longer-time perspective between trust and happiness. In the USA, of those who are not too happy, around three out of four believe they cannot trust other people, whereas those who are happy have a more equal balance between trust and no trust. That those people having trust to a larger degree are happier than other persons is often also the case in the relation between happiness and social relationsor doing voluntary work. Those who within the last 12 months have been working in a voluntary organisation are significantly happier than those who have not.

A feeling of safety when walking in the neighbourhood after dark also has a clear impact on the level of happiness, as shown in Figure 3.4.

Feeling unsafe in one's own local area thus has a clear and negative impact on the level of happiness. Therefore, as will be discussed in Chapter 4, policies that increase the feeling of safety can increase happiness. This is despite the fact that perhaps, for example, more police on the street will not

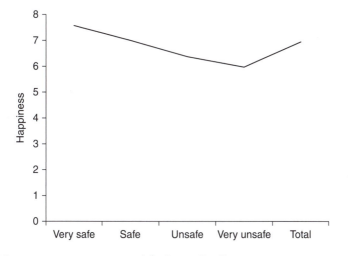

Figure 3.4 Happiness and feeling of safety in 2008.
Source: Based upon European Social Survey (http://nesstar.
ess.nsd.uib.no/webview/) and own calculations.

increase the ability to solve crime, but the increase in the feeling of safety can be an important element for improving the level of happiness (Frey, Leuchinger and Stutzer, 2007).

Those who have never been unemployed are also in general happier than those who have been unemployed and are actively searching for a job. This implies that having a job is an important aspect for individuals as well as societies. It might be important to have many hours of work, although this is not necessarily the case, as shown in Figure 3.5.

Figure 3.5 does not present a clear and single answer to the question on how many hours individuals want to work, although there seems to be a slight indication that it is good to have a job, but not too many hours. The variation also implicitly shows, with working 47 hours per week as an exception, that a lower amount of hours has a positive impact.

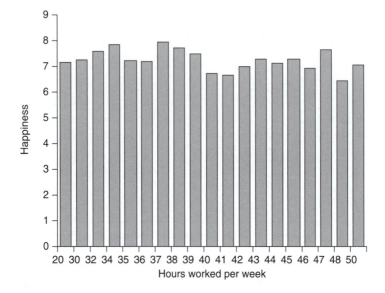

Figure 3.5 Number of hours worked and happiness in Europe. *Source*: Based upon European Social Survey (http://nesstar. ess.nsd.uib.no/webview/) and own calculations.

A possible reason why the relation is less clear could be that in some countries a high number of hours to work is important in order to ensure a "decent" living standard. Furthermore, countries have different institutional structures in the labour market, and different agreements on working conditions. There is also a difference in family structure and tradition, with some countries being more oriented towards male breadwinners whereas, for example, the Nordic countries have a more dual-breadwinner family model.

In general, a higher level of education will imply a higher level of happiness. This might not be the case in all countries, however, as data for the US show that those with a university degree or higher education, or some university education without a degree, have a lower level of happiness, and at the same time those who have completed compulsory elementary education have a higher level than those with incomplete secondary school (Value Surveys Databank). This indicates presumably that it is not only the educational level by itself, but also the ability to use it that is important. However, in the US those in the upper middle class are clearly happier than those in the lower middle class and the working class.

Figure 3.6 shows a country comparison on the average level of happiness in 2008. The figure shows a clear difference in levels of happiness between countries, with Denmark

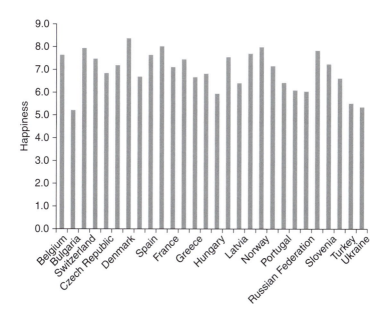

Figure 3.6 Average level of happiness in 2008.
Source: European Social Survey, 4th round, 2008 (http://nesstar.ess.nsd.uib.no/webview/) and own calculations.

having the highest level and Bulgaria and Ukraine having the lowest. Figure 3.6 thus confirms the more general picture of richer nations having a higher level of happiness than poorer nations. The picture might be influenced, though, by the fact that some countries are in transition, and changes, especially unexpected, often have a negative impact on the level of happiness.

In 2008 there was a positive, and significant, relation between level of happiness and how often the individual meets with friends, relatives and colleagues, and a negative, and significant, relation if persons do not have anyone to discuss intimate and personal matters with. This is shown in Figure 3.7 by the relation between social relations and happiness.

The figure shows a clear and very precise relation between the average level of happiness and meeting friends, relatives or colleagues. Those who never meet anyone are clearly less

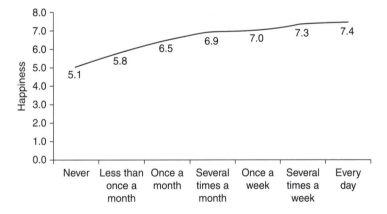

Figure 3.7 Social relations and happiness in Europe, 2008. *Source*: European Social Survey (http://nesstar.ess.nsd.uib. no/webview/).

happy than those with frequent contacts with other people. The differences are less clear, however, when having reached a minimum of at least several times during a month. This is confirmed in other studies where social capital is seen as important for happiness (Leung *et al.*, 2010), which might also be explained by the fact that the sum of a group is larger than the individuals (Haidt *et al.*, 2008). Data for the USA also confirm this picture, even though the questions were related to whether family was important in life. Those who found this important to a lesser degree were also less happy (World Values Surveys Databank, http://www.worldvaluessurvey.org/).

Happiness research might also be used as a way of trying to measure other societal types of development. This has been done, for example, by interpreting that when black people in the USA seem to be much less happy than whites this is an indication of the existence of discrimination (Blanchflower and Oswald, 2002).

SUMMING UP

We are able to measure happiness. Despite the fact that there are and will be methodological issues arising when we try to find out about individuals' level of happiness, the methodological problems with this are not larger than those arising from other types of data collection and analysis that try to depict the individual's position. The ability to be precise might in fact be higher than in qualitative interviews, although these also give other types of information.

A central issue not solved is the way the causality runs. This is, for example, the question of whether happy people are healthier or it is healthy people who are happier. This has still not been possible to deduce. The relation is open for discussion. However, other studies seem to indicate (cf. also Chapter 4) that happy people live longer and thereby also implicitly have better health conditions. Despite the fact that the causality is not always clear and precise, we can use the data on happiness to give an indication of why people are happy and why they are perhaps not happy.

Thus, as shown in this chapter, a higher level of income will, at least until a certain level, improve the level of happiness when we compare across countries. Within countries there might also be a relation to other people's income, implying that it is not only the changes in the individual's income that are important but also their relative position.

The data and figures in this chapter also inform us that there is a relation between several important aspects of daily life for individuals and the level of happiness. This is the case between inequality and life satisfaction, trust in others, social relations with others and, as mentioned above, income in general. The level of education also has an impact in most cases, as also having a job compared with being unemployed has an impact.

The central question will therefore be whether the knowledge about levels of happiness might or will influence our understanding of, and the need for, policy changes. This is the focus of Chapter 4.

APPENDIX: INFORMATION ON THE EUROPEAN SOCIAL SURVEY (http://ess.nsd.uib.no/index.html)

The European Social Survey (the ESS) is a biennial multi-country survey covering over 30 nations. The first round was in 2002/2003 and the fourth in 2008/2009, hence the use of 2002, 2004, 2006 and 2008 in the presentation of data.

The questionnaire used includes two main sections, each consisting of approximately 120 items. There is a "core" module which remains relatively constant from round to round, plus two or more "rotating" modules repeated at intervals. The core module aims to monitor change and continuity in a wide range of social variables: social and public trust; political interest and participation; socio-political orientations; governance and efficacy; moral, political and social values; social exclusion, national, ethnic and religious allegiances; well-being; health and security; human values; demographics; and socio-economics. The changes in modules imply that it is not possible for all years to analyse and combine happiness with all parameters, and each round typically has one or two special modules making a comparison even more difficult.

The fourth round covered the following countries: Belgium, Bulgaria, Croatia, Cyprus, Czech Republic, Denmark, Estonia, Finland, France, Germany, Greece, Hungary, Israel, Latvia, Netherlands, Norway, Poland, Portugal, Romania, Russian Federation, Slovakia, Slovenia, Spain, Sweden, Switzerland, Turkey, Ukraine and the United Kingdom. This combination of countries shows that it covers the north, south, central, east and western Europe. Therefore average data as used in this book, also given the large number of informants, imply a very good knowledge on the situation on average in Europe. More detailed national studies are needed if national positions and developments are to be depicted (cf. for example, Greve, 2010).

4

HAPPINESS AND PUBLIC POLICY
ANY CONNECTION?

INTRODUCTION

That there is a relation between public policy and happiness is not new. This was, for example, formulated in the Beveridge report in 1942, which dealt with what to do with social policy in the UK after the Second World War. There it was described in the following way: "The object of government in peace and in war is not the glory of rulers or of races, but the happiness of the common man." Bhutan wants to combine intervention and a happy society. President Sarkozy in France has asked wise men to write on happiness; and the UK Prime Minister, David Cameron, just to mention one example, also wants to have ways other than classical GDP and economic growth for understanding society's development. This indicates the need for knowing more about whether there is a relation between public policy and happiness and how this can be interpreted.

In general, the literature on happiness agrees that factors such as health, age and marital status are strongly related to the level of happiness, whereas income has an impact to a lesser degree, although richer nations seem to be more happy than poor countries, at least to a certain level (the Easterlin Paradox) (Argyle, 1999; Diener *et al.*, 1999; Fischer, 2009; Frey and Stutzer, 2002a; Leung *et al.*, 2010; Tella *et al.*, 2003; cf. also the data provided in Chapter 3). In the USA the relation to age seems less pronounced than in Europe. More equal societies also tend to be happier, although there might be differences between countries. Individual persons' levels of happiness might also be influenced by other people, and thereby increase the impact and the possible use of public intervention (Layard, 2008). All the elements to a varying degree imply that public intervention might be able to increase the societal level of happiness, although one analysis points to the fact that government spending does not have any significant impact on life satisfaction (Bjørnskov *et al.*, 2007a). There seems, at least in the USA, to be a negative correlation between race and happiness. "Blacks continue to be considerably less satisfied with their lives than whites, although the gap has been cut in half over the last 30 years and seems to grow smaller with age" (Bok, 2010: 16).

The relation between age and happiness is U-shaped (Helliwell, 2003; Oswald, 1997; Peiro, 2006), and part of the reason for this relates to the adaptation of life-styles, and the fact that the good old days in retrospect often look like happy times, although a recent study (Fischer, 2009) indicates that there can be variations in the pattern. Age and happiness are examples of how the relation between the variables might vary across countries, as happiness is also influenced by other contextual factors. Younger people in

Eastern Europe, for example, are much more satisfied than older citizens, which is in contrast to the situation in other countries. Difference in happiness over the life-cycle and how this has an impact on public policy is therefore seemingly also important to understand.

Having a job seems to be important, but so is leisure time. In the USA, for example, leisure activities are enjoyed more than work (OECD, 2009). In some countries religion plays an important role, as does the relation to family and friends. Good health also seems to be important. Other public policy aspects related to happiness include the way the government functions, the degree of corruption, and the effectiveness and stability of government, i.e. trust in the political and administrative system. A low level of corruption in combination with an extensive welfare state can thus have a strong influence. In addition, the impact of voluntary work and civil society on happiness may be included. Housing can be important, but it is questioned whether this is an option for public policy to change in many countries (Clapham, 2010).

A clear paradox that has been pointed out is that sometimes the welfare state is argued to have a responsibility for, among other things, high divorce rates, emotional stress and cultures of dependency (Pacek and Radcliff, 2008). A rise in suicide has been pointed out as a negative impact of modern societies, and thus in contrast to developing a happy society. Why, then, can the state increase happiness through interventions if we are witnessing stress, anxiety and unlucky people (Rothstein, 2010)? Seemingly, this is the fallacy of average thinking and the difference between micro-level development and the macro-societal aspect. As the data in

Chapter 3 and in most studies point to a higher level of well-being due to the welfare state, there is probably a role for societal intervention, although one needs to analyse it carefully.

This chapter will discuss a variety of parameters and their possible influence on the level of happiness in nations, and discuss if happiness can be used as a parameter for policy decisions in welfare states. This is despite the fact that adaptation might imply that policy makers are faced with a hedonic treadmill. Moreover, there is the fact that if higher income alone is no longer able to increase the level of happiness, then it is necessary to pursue other options. The implementation from research to practice might be very difficult, however (Duncan, 2010). Despite this, it can still be positive to inform decision makers about what makes people happy or at least happier (Diener and Seligman, 2004). The parameters chosen reflect the knowledge from existing studies and data in Chapter 3.

One example of a policy instrument that can be discussed is the use of taxes and duties. Taxation of the rich to improve the well-being of the poor can be argued as being based on the moral theory of utilitarianism (Brülde and Bykvist, 2010; Layard, 2005), although it can be used as an argument for taxing the developed countries in order to transfer income to the developing world (Cullis *et al.*, 2010). However, here as in other aspects there might clearly be a conflict between the goal of happiness and other societal goals.

The focus in this chapter will be on what we know about the relationship between central aspects of modern societies and welfare states, including a discussion on how we can understand this type of relationship. This is because a key challenge for public policy is that people's happiness depends on what others have, and is thereby influenced by public decisions (Layard, 2008).

Box 4.1 below presents the main arguments for and against policy interventions based upon the use of the concept of happiness. These different arguments can be seen as central aspects of the difficulty in using happiness as part of policy intervention based upon an ambition to increase happiness. So whether or not one should use this as a parameter for public policy can be discussed, but perhaps it could be right to argue that public policy "should be about enhancing happiness or the welfare of people, now and in the future" (Ng and Ho, 2006: 1). Another reason for using and measuring happiness as a tool in the monitoring of welfare states' development could be that such a measure is non-elitist as it is based on the individual's own perception and evaluation of what a good life is

For	Against
Sufficient knowledge about the conditions of happiness	The measurement of happiness is susceptible to distortion
Happiness can be measured quite accurately	No consensus about the definition of happiness
Happiness has value for us, both final and instrumental	Insufficient knowledge of which policy would increase happiness
Reality has shown that increasing happiness in nations is possible	The promotion of happiness might have negative effects for society and for citizens

Box 4.1 Arguments for and against a politics of happiness

(Rothstein, 2010: 2). Rothstein points out that not all welfare states that are seemingly able to do so, produce happiness for their citizens.

Several of the issues were discussed in Chapter 1: for example, whether measurement of happiness is possible, and the pitfalls related to this type of measurement, including the ceiling effect. Naturally, there might be checks and balances in relation to how to include and use happiness in policy making, because the wish to increase happiness might be at the cost of other societal goals. Still, as included in Box 4.1, we now know a lot about happiness. Furthermore, other types of indicators to be used in policy making can have their flaws.

Another question for policy makers will be whether it can be shown that happiness has a value for individuals and society. However, as already indicated, there might, for example, be a relation between health and happiness, and this will be explored further in "Happiness and health" later in this chapter. Whether or not there is a relation to income will be presented in more detail in "Happiness and income" in the next section. However, it seems clear that, at least on the individual level, for some an increase in income can have a positive impact on their level of happiness.

Some of the core arguments against using happiness in policy making relate to the fact that happiness is a subjective feeling, and that therefore there is no consensus on the definition of happiness. Still, since it is related to the individual it would be difficult to expect one single definition, as it will contain many and very different understandings.

Presumably, we have until now had rather limited knowledge on what type of policy could increase happiness but, as this chapter will show, the knowledge has been increasing in recent years thus helping to show where at least some initiatives can be taken. That a policy for happiness should be paternalistic is in principle not different from any other types of policies, and it might be that the main focus could be on libertarian paternalistic measures (Thaler and Sunstein, 2008). Nudging people to take decisions that would improve their health is thus possible, and better health clearly seems to increase happiness.

The argument that a promotion of happiness should have negative implications rests on the assumption that improvement for some will have negative consequences for others because of, for example, aspiration or envy. This is difficult to estimate and show and, as argued, the comparison of individuals' levels of happiness is difficult.

HAPPINESS AND INCOME

A central question for a policy of happiness is how an increase in income (whether from the public purse or through the labour market or other types of income) will increase the level of happiness. If this also implies that this increase is of a diminishing function, could it imply that a redistribution should be made from rich to poor?

The question to analyse is thus whether there is a relation between income and happiness and, if there is, whether an increase in income will increase the level of happiness. As indicated earlier in the book, there is the so-called Easterlin Paradox that happiness has not increased in many countries despite increases in income. This thesis has been much discussed. The relative position of income will also be taken into consideration, whereas the question of equality will be left mainly to "Happiness and societal development" towards the end of this chapter.

We saw in Chapter 3 that presumably there is a relation between income and happiness. High income countries do in general have a higher level of happiness than low income countries. Still, examples also exist where there is no relation. In Nigeria the average happiness is at the same level as in Italy and Japan (Layard, 2005). The same is the case in Ghana, compared with the UK and Sweden (Delamothe, 2005). Also the old member states of the European Union are more satisfied than the new member states (European Foundation for the Improvement of Living and Working Conditions, 2004a). This comparison is on the societal level. Another analysis showed on a micro-level that life satisfaction was, albeit only slightly, better among the better-off in Calcutta than among poor people, who were better off when looking at social relations (Seligman, 2002a). This can also be put simply as the paradox of happy peasants and miserable millionaires (Graham, 2009).

The implication is that there can be differences at the macro-level and the micro-level, which also implicitly helps to explain why higher income does not necessarily increase the level of happiness. In the literature this is described as being related to comparison, adaptation and aspiration (Schimmel, 2007). These three different elements, although they can work in the same direction, make it possible that increasing income will not increase the individual's happiness.

Throughout history, people have compared themselves with others. This comparison can imply that sometimes people will even prefer to have less income than they could have. This is under the condition that they are still those who have the highest level of income. An experiment at Harvard University showed that students were willing to receive and would prefer a lower level of income if they had a higher income than other persons (Layard, 2005). This may help to explain why, for example, people who could earn more by migrating to another country do not migrate because they risk moving from having a better position than others to having a worse position (Clark *et al.*, 2008). So, despite the fact that economy theory would predict migration based upon wage differentials, this need not be the case. Migrating people might even prefer to come home, not only to be reunited with families, friends and relatives, but also to show that they have a relatively high income.

Comparisons with others have often been seen as part of consumption theory: if others have consumer goods, one will also need to have them. Reference groups are thus important when the individual tries to describe their level of happiness (Smith, 2008). Reference values of others' income might therefore have an impact (Caporale *et al.*, 2007), and average increase in income distributed unevenly can therefore explain a decline or no increase in the level of happiness even in times of increasing average income as measured by GDP.

Comparison can lead to an expectation of achieving higher income and, by this, to be able to buy other goods and services, for example the aspiration of having the newest gadget, music, clothes, etc. Increase in income therefore may make the individual believe that a continued increase in living conditions is possible, including more material goods (Clark *et al.*, 2008; Easterlin, 2001). This may sometimes be labelled "the hedonic treadmill", as achieving one new good will be the rising way to the expectation of being able to achieve another new good.

Aspirations which are not fulfilled, despite an increase in economic consumption possibilities, can lead to a reduced level of happiness. In a sense this reflects what Hirsch originally labelled "positional goods" (Hirsch, 1977).

In line with aspiration is adaptation. One gets used to having a specific level of goods and services, and gradually they are not new but the same and, when you get used to them, their intrinsic value is reduced. When the intrinsic value is reduced this can have a negative influence on happiness. This may have as a consequence that, for example, a pay rise of the same amount per year automatically leads to an expectation that this will continue. A slight reduction in the increase will thereby reduce the level of happiness, although it might still be an increase in the overall real wage level.

Even if there is a relation between happiness and income, the question is whether this is the case in relation to happiness and income inequality. Viewpoints are different, from the one based on data, as in Chapter 3, to the argument that there is a relation, to the viewpoint that no such relations exist (Berg and Veenhoven, 2010). Some have argued, based upon a large survey, that "individuals have a lower tendency to report themselves happy when inequality is high, even after controlling for individual income, a large set of personal characteristics, and year and country" (Alesina *et al.*, 2004, 2009). One problem might be that there are different perspectives on the possibility of coping with inequality around the world. In some countries the belief is that it is possible for all to be rich, whereas in others this might be less pronounced. Europeans might therefore, for example, be more affected by inequality than Americans. This is the case if equality is seen as a luxury good (Alesina *et al.*, 2004). Seemingly, there is an argument for at least some kind of redistribution in order to increase the level of happiness, because a reduced level of inequality increases the social cohesion in countries, and social relations also have a positive impact (cf. "Happiness social relations and other important elements" below). However, this does not inform us about the size of redistribution, and how different levels of change of income and wealth among groups can have different kinds of impact. This is in principle a question for empirical analysis, although it will be very difficult to pursue.

HAPPINESS, SOCIAL RELATIONS AND OTHER IMPORTANT ELEMENTS

In this section, the focus will be on the possible link between happiness and elements such as age, marriage, and visiting and seeing friends and families, and whether the individual feels safe. This will further include the possible link between religion and happiness, as already touched upon earlier. The relation between happiness and voluntary work will be included as this seems to have an impact on happiness (Konow and Earley, 2008).

As already indicated by the figures in Chapter 3, there is a clear indication that social relations have an impact on the level of happiness (Argyle and Martin, 1991; Blanchflower and Oswald, 2002; Lee *et al.*, 1999). Presumably the reason is that social contacts increase the likelihood of not being alone, having positive feelings for others and being valued as an individual. Hence the ability to have and establish social networks, i.e. social capital, is an important aspect of a happy society (Helliwell, 2003).

Married people in general seem to be happier than single and divorced people. The causal relation is not completely clear, whether happy people are more likely than non-happy people to get married, or whether it is marriage that makes people happier. Despite the lack of this knowledge, one could imagine that a marriage bonus might be offered, for example paying a couple a cash or tax benefit each year that they stay married (Weisbach, 2007). This naturally might imply a high deadweight loss due to the fact that many presumably will stay married anyhow. However, it is an indication that a policy to ensure happiness might be possible.

Visiting friends and family and having personal relations has a positive impact for the individual. Establishing personal relations has presumably not been seen as a goal of the welfare state but, on the other hand, help to encourage social contact by supporting voluntary work in different ways (cf. also below, the possible positive impact of this in itself), or by making it easier for people to meet and engage in activities that offer social contacts is another issue. Support for sport, for example, might be argued to be important not only in relation to helping better health, but also as a way of supporting contact with others. Therefore, activities which might not be seen as natural for state support, given that the market in principle can supply it and no market failure has occurred as a reason to support it, if they fulfil several purposes can be useful in order to increase the level of happiness. Social contact can appear to have a positive impact on earnings (European Commission, 2009), although the causality is not necessarily certain.

Age and happiness seems to have a U-shape: high in the young age group, declining in middle age, and then again increasing in old age. Especially when adjusting for income the U-shape is clear. It is further so that "it is not ageing as such which results in declining happiness, but rather the circumstances associated with ageing" (Lelkes, 2008: 1). When young the world is still open, and when reaching the age of retirement one has a clearer knowledge of what is possible and what is not possible, which has an impact on the level of happiness. The shape can be different, and a recent OECD analysis implies that the curve can be slightly different (Fischer, 2009).

Religious people, is is often argued, have in general a higher level of happiness than non-religious people. However, the latest European Social Survey indicates that those who do not belong to a religious group are slightly happier than those who belong (7.1 compared with 6.9). Even asking differently whether people are very religious or not gives the same information. Those who say they are not at all religious are slightly happier than those who are very religious (again, 7.1 compared with 6.9). The difference is not significant, however. This indicates that religion, seemingly at least in Europe today, has a less clear and less significant role than has been shown in more classical analyses of happiness (Lelkes, 2006b). The picture in the USA is different; those who attend a religious service at least once a week are happier than those who attend less often. Almost half are very happy, whereas it is around one out of four or five of those who attend only on special days and less often than once a year (World Values Surveys Databank, 2006, http://www.worldvaluessurvey.org/). This is an indication of how different societies can react and have different relations between happiness and important societal aspects.

Whether or not those participating in voluntary work are happier than others is an open question. An argument could be made that when participating there is connection to other people and it gives rise to the "do-good feeling". There is actually a rather large difference, so on average those who have been working in another organisation within the last 12 months reach a value of 7.7 compared with 6.8 for those not participating. This indicates that doing voluntary work can influence the individual's level of happiness. Again the question might be, "What is the cause and what is the effect?" Is it the voluntary worker who gains an increase in the level of happiness as this implies a purpose in life, for example something to do? See also "Happiness and the labour market" (in the following section) on the big bad wolf syndrome, or is it possibly that happy people have more energy and do more activities?

Altruism is positively related with health for women and with well-being for both men and women, and, seemingly, "adults who engage in altruistic social interest behaviours experience better mental health and have lower mortality rates than non-altruistic adults" (Schwartz *et al.*, 2008: 1). Nevertheless, this is an indication that voluntary work might have a value in itself even if it is only helping those actually doing voluntary work.

Married people are in general happier than divorced or people living as singles, which can be explained at least partly by the fact that this includes more close social relations than being a single person. Whether happy people are more likely to be married, or whether it is the social relations related to being married, cannot be answered. Presumably the link can go in different directions. Divorced or single people can have a reduced level of happiness, either due to having lost a close person or feeling left after the divorce. Given the U-shape function of happiness over life, it seems that a recovery of the level of happiness takes place.

"The winner takes it all" is by now a common understanding, as well as the title of a famous song from the Swedish pop group ABBA. The literature shows that the winner is happy, at least for a short while. However, winning a silver medal might not give rise to the same level of happiness as the individual/team has been close to being the best, and it therefore might give rise to the feeling of having lost. Being number 3 and winning a bronze medal therefore often implies a higher level of happiness than winning silver.

Whether the fact that those who lose a game have a reduced level of happiness implies that we should reduce the number of people losing is another question. A football match with no winners might sometimes be a good match for a spectator; however, people watching often prefer to see a winner. So, it will be difficult for society to intervene in this type of development, although there might be a need to emphasise that all persons cannot be winners at the same time.

The need to be a winner can help in explaining why so many lotteries have a large number of small prizes. They know that people prefer a sure gain instead of an unsure loss, even if this implies that they in fact then will reduce their overall chance of higher income. Loss has a more negative impact on individuals than gain, also labelled prospect theory (Frey and Stutzer, 2002b). Therefore reducing the risk of losing even a small amount of money can be important for the individual.

The reason that some continue to play with the hope of winning a large prize is that the dream of being able to do exactly what they would like to do makes people happy. Sometimes, it seems even that the dream is better that the prize in itself. This might help to explain why lottery winners are not happier than people who have not been able to win (Konow and Early, 2008). Another explanation of why winning has only a temporary impact on happiness is, as described in Chapter 2, that we adapt to our level, which is the case with a sudden increase in income.

HAPPINESS AND THE LABOUR MARKET

In the following, the focus will be on whether having a job will increase our happiness or whether we will be happier being outside the labour market. The relation between unemployment and happiness is thus part of the analysis in this section. Furthermore, even having a job might not be the whole story. People might want to have a job but not work more hours, and there might also be a relation between well-being and job satisfaction. If this is the case, then this can have an impact on our understanding of why policies to improve this might be important for individuals and companies as well as societies.

Naturally, it might be that the relation between happiness and the labour market is not the same in all countries, depending on the structure of jobs and the labour market. There is, at the least, seemingly a difference between Europe and the USA (Okulicz-Kozaryn, 2010).

However, the general perception is that individuals in Europe, as well as those in the USA, who have a job are happier than those who do not have a job (Tella and MacCulloch, 2008). Being unemployed seems to have a negative impact on the degree of happiness (Clark and Oswald, 1994), and it may be argued that "unemployment seems to be the prime source of unhappiness" (Oswald, 1997: 1828). There is a study that even indicates that those without work have a 12-times higher than average risk of attempting suicide, this is especially so for the long-term unemployed (Oswald, 1997). In the USA, those having a full-time job are happier than those having a part-time job, although the difference in happiness between full-time workers and the unemployed is not significant. Furthermore, those retired from the labour market were those with the highest frequency of being very happy in the USA in 2006 (data from World Values Surveys Databank, 2006, http:// www.worldvaluessurvey.org/). The data for part-time work are, however, based upon a very limited number of answers and therefore are not significant.

The comparison between countries also indicates this relation, as it is, for example, shown in comparison of OECD as well as EU countries (Alesina *et al.*, 2004; European Foundation for the Improvement of Living and Working Conditions, 2004a, 2004b; OECD, 2006). One study indicates that no significant effect can be shown, while also referring to several studies that have shown that a relation exists (Peiro, 2006). To a larger degree, happy people are "more likely to secure a job, more likely to receive favourable evaluations from their supervisors, more likely to find their job meaningful, less likely to lose their job, quicker to be re-employed if they do" (Kesebir and Diener, 2008: 71).

Individuals, at the same time, especially in more affluent societies, highly value their spare time. In the USA, working is ranked 11th out of 13 activities. The comparison included relaxing, eating, socialising (both at work and after work), and working was only rated higher than commuting to and from work (OECD, 2009). This is an important reminder that, although a job is important, other domains of life are, at least in more affluent societies, also important.

Therefore, even though people in employment are happier than others, one cannot deduce from this that working more will make people even happier. On the contrary, the long history in all western countries seems to indicate that when becoming richer, increased wealth also implies less work, which also perhaps helps to explain why richer societies are happier than less-rich societies; and it might even be that the number of hours worked has a significant and negative effect on happiness (Tella and MacCulloch, 2008). The data in Chapter 3 indicate that there can be variations among countries, which can be explained by the difference in the level of wealth, so that in richer countries the willingness to work more will be reduced compared with countries with a lower living standard. Free time and the ability to choose this can thus have an impact on the level of happiness.

Work is important not only as a way to achieve income, but also to acquire social status, connection with other people, having friends, doing something important (perhaps for others), or just having something to do. This has been labelled the "big bad wolf" syndrome (Hylland Eriksen, 2008). The big wolf in the fairytales always wanted to chase the three little pigs and eat them. One day he actually succeeded, but while he was on the way to cook the three little pigs, the little wolf asked him what then he would do tomorrow. Realising that it was his life project to find ways to catch the three little pigs the wolf released them – although presumably with regret after having thought about being able to find other life projects. Still, this is an indication that we need and like to have a purpose in life.

The negative impact of unemployment is reduced if the level of unemployment is high (Winkelmann, 2008), since more people will be in the same situation, and thereby being unemployed is more a societal than an individual problem. The negative impact of being unemployed can only be compensated by "an enormous amount of extra income" (Oswald, 1997: 1821). This can be explained by the fact that work is not only done to earn an income but, as described above, it also implies social relations and, as shown in "Happiness, social relations and other important elements" in the previous section, they are important for the individual.

A problem related to the labour market, as already touched upon in the section on income, is that we might have our well-being reduced if other people receive a wage increase we thought we should have had ourselves. Relative comparisons thus matter in the labour market. Therefore, wage bargaining at the local level can be counterproductive to a happier society, and the balance between wages for different groups is therefore very important. Even receiving less income, although presumably in rare cases, might imply a higher level of satisfaction if other persons get less.

Happy people are presumably more effective, as it is argued that "greater employee well-being is associated with better job performance, lower absenteeism, and reduced job turnover, and is therefore of particular interest to firms and other organizations" (Frey and Stutzer, 2002b: 29). The relation between well-being and worker productivity also implies that the quality of jobs "can be used to guide business decisions to improve performance, productivity and profitability" (Diener *et al.*, 2009: 168). This will not be explored in further detail here, but given the many companies that employ human resources staff this is an indication of the importance attached to this aspect, and that good quality of jobs can be a win-win situation for the individuals, society and business.

The relation between well-being and employment thus not only relates to extrinsic factors (such as wage, status, number of hours of work) but also intrinsic factors (such as quality of the work, stress, interesting work opportunities etc.). The intrinsic factors seemingly have a high impact on happiness (Waterman *et al.*, 2008). If happy people are more effective, as indicated above, then it will be a win-win situation to ensure more happy workers, as they are both more productive and happy at the same time. "Happy workers are better organizational citizens, meaning that they help other people at work in various ways" (Diener and Seligman, 2004: 1). For society this will increase wealth and in those areas where the government might be able to help this could therefore be a policy area to do something about.

HAPPINESS AND HEALTH

Will happy people live longer and be healthier than unhappy people, or is it that those who are healthier are also happier? Which way the causality is running is thus important. However, first it is important to try to find out whether any relation can be traced. Several studies seem to indicate that happy people live longer. Health shows a clear and systematic relationship with happiness (Anand and Clark, 2006; Peiro, 2006; Schimmel, 2007; Veenhoven, 1991, 2008b). It can be expressed as follows: "health is a major component of [an] individual's subjective well-being" (Lelkes, 2006a: 290). Based on data for 49 countries and three rounds of the World Values Survey (http://www.worldvaluessurvey.org/), being in very good health compared with good health increases the happiness level by 0.52. It appears that to be in very poor health rather than ill health reduces the level of happiness by 0.46. On the 10-point scale often used, this means a difference in health status from the best to the worst subjectively assessed health level is a difference of 2.46 percentage points (Helliwell, 2003). Another study has shown that there is a correlation between blood pressure and happiness, and concludes that "happier nations report fewer blood-pressure problems" (Blanchflower and Oswald, 2008: 220). This was what was shown in the data used in Chapter 3, that people with a positive subjective evaluation of their health were happier than others.

Despite this, virtually all studies show that happiness and age have a U-shaped relationship as already mentioned. We are most fortunate as adolescents and in older age, and less during the interim period, although there may be variations depending on the specific context and historical/economic development. This means that even in a phase of life where health is less good the single individual is fundamentally more satisfied with his or her life than in times where their health objectively is better. Several reasons can explain this kind of relation.

One type of explanation relates to the problem of measurements in relation to health that optimistic people may have a tendency to assess their health more positively than it really is (Helliwell, 2003). Another explanation for the correlations between age and happiness is presumably linked with people's ability to adapt to their surroundings. There is, as with income, a certain improvement in happiness levels related to the number of life years, and this perhaps also explains why poorer health in later life has a lesser impact.

Another possible explanation is that, despite the fact that most gradually suffer poorer health throughout life and are able to do less than in the younger years, the higher degree of happiness can be linked with the understanding of life and society (and the understanding of oneself, one's surroundings and opportunities) which increases through the life cycle. This increase in the individual's self-understanding helps to explain why they find they have a higher quality of life (Yang, 2008). Another way to interpret this is that it is not necessarily getting older, which for some may cause a slight decrease in the level of satisfaction, but rather the circumstances associated with getting older, for example fewer options and reduced ability to live without any hindrance in daily life.

Studies have shown that even for people who have been the victim of a serious accident, and thus became severely disabled, it is possible that happiness can return to almost the same level as before (Frey and Stutzer, 2002b; Kacapyr, 2008). This is despite the fact that most people are unlikely to wish to be in this type of situation. Other research finds, however, that serious illness or permanent disability has negative and lasting effects on happiness (Graham, 2008). There is a difference in how severe the changes are. The likelihood of returning to a previous level of happiness is greater if the changes have been relatively modest. Conversely, large changes due to, for example, extensive disability mean that the probability of returning to the previous level is weaker (Oswald and Powdthavee, 2006).

Whether health is the factor that makes some people more optimistic than others can be difficult to assess, but apparently optimists live longer than others: "[the] optimist's life is about eight years longer than [the] pessimist's" (Schimmel, 2007: 10). Happier people will therefore be able to live longer and happier lives. The observed positive effect on life expectancies of happy people is stable and represents between 7.5 and 10 years under a series of studies. Whether it is 7 or 10 extra years that happy people live longer can be difficult to determine, and it is not always possible to find that happier people live so many years longer (Veenhoven, 2008b). Life satisfaction among 75–84-year-old people predicts their mortality, whereas it does not apply to persons over 84 years (Diener and Seligman, 2004).

It is thus difficult to measure the correlation between happiness and longevity, where all the various factors that may affect length of life are included, but it emphasises that there may be a correlation between the degree of happiness, longevity and health. It may be that happy people live more healthily, are more receptive to public information, more aware of disease symptoms or that there are a number of other possible interactions with other factors.

One survey (Box 4.2), however, seems to emphasise that people with more positive emotions than others live longer, even assuming that they also have the same type of life, same nutrition, etc. There is still no study to examine whether differences in genetic factors may have an impact.

The famous nun study is based on reading the autobiographies of 180 nuns in Milwaukee, Wisconsin, and Baltimore, Maryland in the USA. They were written when the nuns were on average 22 years old. All the autobiographies were written in the early 1930s, and therefore the analysis is based on historical data and is thus not affected by the rationalisation of how the life cycle has been. Comparison between average life expectancy and positive emotions in these autobiographies proved to be significant. Those who were most positive lived longer than other nuns, when their mortality was studied around 60 years later and onwards (Danner, Snowdon and Friesen, 2001).

The nuns had lived the same type of life, had the same type of diet, etc., so that there is a good opportunity for comparison and less risk that outside factors, apart from possible genetic differences, may have affected the outcome of the investigation.

Box 4.2 Nun study – relationship between positive emotions and a long life.

People with a high degree of social capital (see also the section on social relations) seem to live longer than those with a lower degree of social capital (Field, 2008). There may therefore be a risk that the factors that contribute to reducing social relationships can have a negative impact on happiness. One study found, for example, that watching more television could reduce social relations ("relations goods") and thereby affect the individual's happiness adversely. Watching TV seemingly pushed social contacts away or made them less frequent than before, and thus reduced the level of happiness (Bruni and Stanca, 2008).

The relationship between social capital and better health can be influenced by various factors. One factor may be that the network itself contributes to a healthier lifestyle, including greater attention from others which encourages one to undergo necessary tests earlier. At the same time, social networks can help people to be in a better position to press for putting in place the necessary examinations and treatments in health care. Another factor may be that groups with high social capital generally seem to have a higher income. The interaction between a number of factors can thus influence the outcome, and when there is an accumulation of factors this might have great importance for assessing health and happiness.

Happy people must be assumed to be less prone to depression. A study has shown that changes in the number of suicides – both upwards and downwards – move opposite to trends in happiness (Tella *et al.*, 2003). In other words, the evolution of a society's happiness affects the number of suicides; and the positive correlation between happiness and health is stronger in relation to mental health (Graham,

2008). Whether it is possible to change the number of people with depression by offering special training in what makes the individual happy is more doubtful, though there are people who believe that depression may be affected in this way. As an example, an experiment which attempted to get people to fill a web exercise (three blessings), resulted in 94 per cent of the highly depressed being less depressed, and 92 per cent were happier – even compared with a control group they were less depressed one year later (http:// newsvote.bbc.co.uk/mpapps). The argument is that it is important to talk about positive emotions and focus on strengths instead of talking about problems. This may be reflected in modern management, with its focus on challenges instead of problems.

Despite the fact that happy people are less depressed than others, this is not an indication that a modern welfare state does not have any risk of suicides or increasing numbers of people living with stress. The average can improve and at the same time for some people there might be an increase in the daily pressure.

Others find, however, that although social networks can reduce stress and thus perhaps also the risk of mental illness, this seems not to be documented – for example there is no clear and unambiguous link between happiness and this type of disease (Field, 2008).

One problem in such studies is whether it is the current behaviour that affects happiness, or whether long-term factors may have a larger impact. For example, a US study showed that "91 per cent of participants who did not perceive themselves to have had warm relationships with their mothers had diagnosed midlife diseases (coronary artery disease, high blood pressure, duodenal ulcer, and alcoholism)" (Post, 2005: 67). Although this is a single study with a limited number of participants, it is concluded that it is now based on a "widely accepted biopsychosocial model that being loved, cared for and supported by others is critically important to health and treatment efficacy" (ibid.). This further stresses the need to look at long-term intervention and not only short-term happiness to create greater satisfaction and longer life in a community.

In conclusion, this indicates that "happiness therefore seems to add years to life, as well as life to years" (Delamothe, 2005: 1490). This could in general be an argument for public intervention and to try to help people become happier and to look at the number of happy years as a yardstick for how countries look and evolve. One definition is:

Number of years happy = life expectancy at birth × (0–1) happiness level.

(Veenhoven, 2008c)

Note: where 0–1 is a conversion of the measurement of happiness and happiness level is based upon answers in surveys.

If, for example, a scale of 1–10 is used, as in many of the studies used in this book, a value of 6 is equal to that which is multiplied by 0.6 and a value of 8 to 0.8. The number of happy years calculated in this way, for instance, is 62.9 in Switzerland and only 12.5 in Zimbabwe. In a rich country such as Japan, people have a long life expectancy, but their degree of happiness is not high (Veenhoven, 2008c).

The relation between happiness and health thus implies that if instruments can be found to increase happiness this will have a positive impact on health and, thereby, presumably on the cost of health care. If the relation is the other way around, then an increase in health achieved by policy interventions will increase happiness. Thus a ban on smoking can improve happiness on average even if it reduces it for heavy smokers. Nudging people to eat more healthily by presenting for the healthy elements in shops and cafeterias first could therefore imply a win-win situation (Thaler and Sunstein, 2008). If the workplace can be safer or reduce pressure on the individuals this could also imply a higher level of happiness.

This has implications for the educational system, assuming that an increase in exercise and sport brings a more satisfying life (Bok, 2010) and, at the same time, a more active life brings better health. Thus the support or integration of physical elements in the educational system can increase a society's level of happiness.

Increasingly, there has been an awareness that a soft paternalistic approach – especially by setting the default options in such a way that decisions which are good for society and individuals are taken without any strong type of intervention being used in order to achieve it – can have a positive impact (Loewenstein and Ubel, 2008).

Seemingly, happy people live longer due to the fact that they are happy, so policies implying a happy life can be worthwhile to pursue, although they will have to compete for the scarce economic resources available for public sector intervention.

HAPPINESS AND SOCIETAL DEVELOPMENT

This section will probe into the relation between happiness and how society develops, including trust in the political system (cf. the data in Chapter 3). To put it another way, trust might replace suspicion and fear and thereby have a positive impact on happiness (Bok, 2010; Helliwell, 2003). This analysis will not include income, as this was discussed in "Happiness and income" in the early part of this chapter. It will include whether or not a goal of income equality is important for a society with an ambition to increase the level of happiness. Furthermore, societal development today seems influenced by the level of education and ability to ensure life-long learning even more than before. Thus, one question is whether education might have an impact on the level of happiness, thereby implying a win-win situation by investing in education. A richer and happier society can be the outcome. The possible relation between welfare benefits and happiness will also be included.

One analysis, for example, has indicated that more generous unemployment benefits increase the level of happiness (Tella and MacCulloch, 2008). This is a clear indication of how social policy has an impact on a society's level of happiness. The rationale behind it is that when entitled to a more generous level of benefits the individual will have a higher level of economic security in case of, for example, becoming redundant, so even if this does not fully reduce the negative impact of being unemployed, a high replacement rate helps.

National well-being can thus be promoted in a variety of ways, and one of those can be international sports events. One study showed only a positive significant impact of hosting football events; however, as the authors also point out, the analysis is based on European nations where football is the dominant sport (Kavetsos and Szymanski, 2010).

This is just as a reminder of how well-being can be promoted not only with traditional goods, but also through the development of activities that make us feel good.

Societies have instruments that might improve the level of happiness. This chapter has not tried to evaluate and judge the various options, merely to point to certain possible options. There will be a need to evaluate the potential increase in the level of happiness and the cost associated with it, including whether the improvement will be at the expense of other persons' happiness, as the chapter has not discussed inequality in happiness in detail, but only how this relates on average.

Inequality in happiness might, but need not, be related to the degree of equality in a country. An analysis based upon 78 countries for the years around 2000 (Ott, 2005) showed, for example, that:

- High level of happiness and low inequality in happiness could be found in the Netherlands.
- Low level of happiness and low inequality in happiness could be found in Pakistan.
- High level of happiness and high inequality in happiness could be found in South Africa.
- Low level of happiness and high equality of happiness could be found in Russia.

Still, the public sector's role can be only of a limited nature in relation to inequality in happiness, unless interventions that improve happiness or equality in general also imply a change in the degree of inequality in happiness. This could, for example, be an increase in the health conditions in societies, as well as a higher degree of economic security, as a higher level of economic security (by generous welfare benefits) and longer life-expectancy seems to increase the level of happiness.

Trust has been mentioned as an element to improve happiness, and this also seems to be the case if political stability exists (Argyle, 1987; Frey and Stutzer, 2002a, 2002b). Reduction of corruption and a stable democratic system with clear knowledge about, and stability in, decision making can thus have a positive impact on individuals' lives. In this way, a state that ensures that corruption is at the lowest possible level will enhance the well-being of its citizens (Bok, 2010). A possible reason why trust might have such an important impact is that a high level of social trust seemingly has a relation to factors such as "tolerance toward minorities, participation in public life, and education, health and subjective well-being" (Rothstein, 2010: 19).

The level of inequality is in most cases considered as an element having an impact on happiness, although for an exception see Veenhoven (2010). However, there might be differences between countries, such as, for example, "Europeans have a stronger aversion to inequality than Americans have" (Frey and Stutzer, 2002a: 412). The main reason for the relation has to do with elements such as comparisons, as described in Chapter 2, but also aspiration to have the options and opportunities others have. There are further moral and philosophical arguments related to the discussion on equality and inequality that not will be included here. Furthermore, one could discuss inequality in the level of happiness and whether or not public policy has a role to play regarding trying to ensure a just distribution of the level of happiness. However, given the varied nature of what makes the individual happy that is difficult to achieve and regulate, such as the interpersonal comparison mentioned in Chapter 2. However, in so far as the welfare state can help in ensuring more equal life chances and have an impact on happiness, then there might be a relation between policy intervention of the welfare state and the degree of equality in happiness.

Inequalities have negative impacts on several societal issues and can thereby be important for the level of happiness, even if it is not possible to discern that a simple relation exists, by its impact on other elements of society's development. Health, for example, is seemingly better in more equal societies, and social relations are better and crime is less frequent in more equal societies (Wilkinson, 2006).

That social capital has an important impact on societal development, and therefore that there is a need to measure it, can be witnessed by the fact that the EU-SILC data have elements enabling the estimation of social capital. One is based on contact with relatives, another on contact with friends, and also the number of organisations, clubs, etc. to which one belongs. The relation based on these data confirms that the Nordic countries especially fare better than the other EU member states (European Commission, 2009).

Social capital is related to the level of education and, further, "the evidence that learning promotes well-being is overwhelming" (Field, 2009 p. 5) – although not to the same degree in all countries (cf. for example, the data for the USA in Chapter 3). Learning and education thus promote happiness, and presumably do so in a variety of ways. One is that participation in education (especially for adults) increases the likelihood of having friends and someone to talk to, and an increase in the level of social networks, although here also the causal direction can be difficult to establish.

Social capital can improve a government's performance by ensuring more co-operation and consensus and thereby helping to increase trust in society, for example, as shown for the USA (Knack, 2000). Finally, as social capital can be influenced by effective and impartial bureaucracies (Rothstein and Stolle, 2007), this implies an impact of the public administration on happiness. A public administration built upon fairness, lack of discrimination and less corruption will imply a movement towards a higher level of happiness in a society. Thus, once again, this implies that the state and the way it functions have an impact on a society's level of happiness.

The welfare state and social policy intervention can be important for societal development, and therefore it can be important to analyse the impact of spending on social policy. One analysis tends to argue that social spending has no significant impact on life satisfaction (Bjørnskov *et al.*, 2007a); however, the data used do not include subsidies and transfers and, therefore, the conclusion can be questioned. Furthermore, it can be questioned whether the sole focus should be on spending instead of the possible impact on issues such as inequality, employment and better health. Based upon analysis of nine European countries, it seems that social policy has a positive impact on happiness (Greve, 2010), or as expressed in one of the articles in the book (Greve, 2010): "The best argument in favour of the welfare state seems to be its positive effect on average levels of happiness" (Fors, 2010, with reference to Pacek and Radcliff, 2008).

A further reason might in fact be as indicated implicitly by Barr, that the welfare state is the most effective means to ensure collective welfare as the administrative cost of universal programmes can be less than individual insurance-based programmes (Barr, 2001).

SUMMING UP

Policy makers do have a role to play in relation to the level of happiness in modern societies. It is not always an easy role, given that people adapt, thus implying a risk of policy makers ending up in a hedonic treadmill constantly trying to give people more, and then they will expect even more.

However, there can be some elements that are more important than others. Improving the health of citizens can, for example, be one important element. Ensuring a high degree of social security can be another element, as security (both economically and personally) is important for the individual's level of happiness. Obviously, policy makers are faced with a dilemma that they have to make priorities because citizens also prefer to have their own individualistic approach. This implies a balance between interventions and options for choice of the citizens. Still, ways of improving employment and job security are important for most people and can thus enhance happiness. This implies that a "reasonable" replacement rate in the case of unemployment can be important as part of making society happier.

Feelings of security might not only be in relation to economic security. The feeling of security in the street or at home also has an impact on the level of happiness. Despite the fact that, for example, more police on the streets do not have any effect on the level of crime, their presence might have a positive impact on the level of happiness. Thus, if increasing the level of happiness is at the centre of policy making, this can be a reason to increase the visible police presence.

Social relations are important for many people. The welfare state cannot ensure social relations, but it might support the structures in society so that this is more easily achieved and thereby increase the level of happiness. Furthermore, it might be a reason for supporting voluntary work, given that this increases social relations, and support does not need to be based upon the expectation that voluntary work in itself is important.

Investment in education and further education can have an impact in several ways. One is due to the fact that educated people are seemingly happier, but also that they have lower risk of unemployment and in general are healthier than others. Education seems to bring about more social contact and a better network. Life-long learning is no longer only necessary in order to improve the match between demand and supply in the labour market, but also because it will improve happiness.

Given that both marriage and having a job make people happier, this is an argument for supporting the ability to combine work and family life. The ambition, for example, in the EU to have affordable and high-quality day care can seemingly not only be justified as increasing the labour supply and equality between men and women in relation to their access to the labour market, but also as increasing happiness in society. Welfare spending, seen in this light, is therefore an investment in a happier society.

However, there might be a risk if the way of improving happiness to a large degree is to use force instead of libertarian paternalism, and it could be argued that "people must be able to opt out easily from new policies" (Haidt *et al.*, 2008). This can be a conflict between deciding important aspects of society's development that might be in conflict with individual preferences. However, this has for a long time been an issue in how to develop societies.

The welfare states can, at least to a certain degree, help to improve happiness by a combination of social policy while, at the same time, increasing the general level of wealth in society. Given that higher income, at least to a certain degree, increases the level of happiness, policy makers are faced with the challenge to fulfil and have an economic growth policy that increases well-being. Whether well-being alone can be measured by an increase in economic factors such as GDP is doubtful, and this implies a need for new measures of welfare. This is the focus of the next chapter.

5

WHY WE NEED A NEW MEASUREMENT OF WELFARE

INTRODUCTION

Modern welfare states have often been evaluated based upon GDP per capita as the best indicator of the different countries' positions in the world economic order and the level of welfare. Growth in GDP has further been seen as a central parameter for economic development.

There have been serious criticisms that using GDP as the measurement is flawed (Frey and Stutzer, 2002b). This might explain why some argue that "happiness research is merely the latest in the long line of criticism of the concept of GNP" (Johns and Ormerod, 2007: 52). This chapter will explore whether it is possible to include happiness in the understanding of countries' economic and social development and just indicate how the score of such measure is compared between countries.

New types of measuring progress, for example, national accounts of well-being, will be included in the presentation.

This can be of importance so that when making decisions it is not only the possible short-term impact on the economic system that should be looked upon as part of the decision, but also the impact more generally on well-being.

Gross national happiness has been one type of alternative measure to analyse society's development. Canada even has a law, the Well-being Measurement Act, with the aim of publishing information regarding "the economic, social and environmental well-being of people, communities and ecosystems in Canada" (Tella and MacCulloch, 2008: 23). In New Zealand, there is a Ministry which has responsibility for a social well-being survey (Duncan, 2005). In both France and the UK, as indicated earlier, there has been a growing interest in other types of measurement of societal development.

The United Nations has developed other types of indexes, such as the Human Poverty Index, the Gender Empowering Index and a Human Development Index. The last includes elements such as life expectancy and illiteracy as well as GDP. This is just another indication of how, when measuring and understanding society's development, it is important to see it in a broader perspective. Furthermore, the OECD has increasingly used and presented data on well-being and other non-monetary indicators.

This indicates that the discussion is not just an academic discussion, but is also related to decision making. This chapter will explore, first, why GDP is not sufficient to measure the well-being of a society, and thereafter to discuss whether we can find new ways of measuring society's development, including a presentation of some of the ways that have emerged in recent years.

WHY IS GDP NOT SUFFICIENT?

GDP has been criticised for a long time for not been suffi-cient to describe societal development as, for example, an increase in the number of traffic accidents also increases the level of GDP (at least in the short run due to increased activ-ities in the health care sector). This problem of measuring GDP has been known for many years (see, for example, Nordhaus and Tobin, 1973). Recent years have seen further interest in how economic growth and sustainable develop-ment could be combined. GDP is thus seemingly in need of a change in relation to classical measurements of a society's welfare. It describes development at a macro level only and thus has low external validity (Diener and Seligman, 2004), and no ability to measure individuals' satisfaction or happi-ness. Still, it is also argued that at least it gives a good starting point for the evaluation of a society and its development, and that there is a consistency in the different approaches to measuring society's development (Boarini *et al.*, 2006; OECD, 2006).

The size of GDP related to public sector interventions is measured based upon input (for example the amount of money spent on welfare issues) but not the outcome of the different kinds of interventions. Therefore, for example, public sector interventions to improve the environment or health of a popu-lation also include in the measurement the direct cost, whereas the long-term impact on health or the environment, even though health has a positive impact on happiness, is not included in the measurement. To put it another way: "Even worse, GDP increases when convivial reciprocity is replaced by anonymous market relations and when rising crime, pollution, catastrophes, or health hazards trigger defensive or repair expenditures" (Fleurbaey, 2009: 1029).

Many activities in society which are not part of market or government activities are thus not included in the analysis. The hidden economy and its size, which can be large in some countries, are not included in such measures. Economic interventions moving activities from the hidden economy to the open economy might look like an increase in wealth at the macro level in the statistics, but will not have changed income at the micro level. Services within the household, voluntary social work and interactions between friends are not included in classical measurements as discussed by Frey and Stutzer (2002a), who also indicate that the level of GDP per capita does not show the distribution of income or, as described in Chapter 2, the relative position, aspiration and adaptation of individuals. This has implications for the level of happiness and therefore is an argument for why GDP per capita is not a sufficient measure to use when trying to describe societal development.

This was the basis for the recommendation from the report to the French President that there was a need to "*shift emphasis from measuring economic production to measuring people's well-being*" [italics as in the report] (Stiglitz *et al.*, 2009: 12). Robert F. Kennedy is often quoted as having said about GNP that: "It measures everything, in short, except that which makes life worthwhile."

However, even if we agree that GNP as well as GDP is not a sufficient or precise instrument to measure society's development, this does not by itself inform us about what to include in the measurement, and what kind of flaws this kind of measurement will have. The next section will look into this, but it highlights why the measurement of happiness has been a growth area given that this, to some extent, can explain and inform us about the development and status of other elements and aspects of society's core values.

OTHER ELEMENTS TO BE INCLUDED IN THE ANALYSIS

Historically, social scientists have been interested in measuring aspects of societal life other than economic development. In the 1960s and 1970s, social indicator research was an attempt to include in the understanding of societal development aspects not only related to objective, and thereby relatively simple, ways of measuring well-being, but also how to measure and analyse subjective well-being (Allardt, 2003).

Research into subjective well-being tried to establish indicators which could measure new areas. This included elements such as satisfaction, access to social resources, social relations and understanding of how societies function (European Foundation for the Improvement of Living and Working Conditions, 2003). The revival of social indicators took place with work, among other places, at the OECD (2005), and then regularly in the book series *Societies at a Glance*. These books focus on self-sufficiency, equality, health and social cohesion, and the social indicator research as developed by the OECD has increased the awareness that aspects other than classical monetary ones are important. Data on life expectancy are just one example, but the ability to finance and pay for basic amenities can be another, and social relations is another central issue of which to be aware.

The focus in social indicator research shows why not just objective factors are important in the measurement and reporting on how a country is developing. It is also important to know, and be aware of, how individuals feel about and look upon their life situations.

In the USA, indicators in line with this have been in core areas such as crime, the environment, education and governance – including measures such as: violent crime rate, level of sulphur dioxide in the air, participation in organised sports, rates of volunteering, attendance at performing arts, home ownership, enrolment in science and engineering, adolescent birth rate, and labour force participation (Diener *et al.*, 2009: 24). Diener and colleagues also point to several domains where using and implementing the measurement of indicators could be important, such as in relation to material goods, health, productivity, security, intimacy, community and spirituality.

This is not to say that there are no problems related to the use and measurement of subjective indicators (Hoorn, 2008). These include how to do the aggregation, as discussed earlier in relation to happiness, as well as the choice of indicators. That is the reason why there might be divergent views on which type of index to use, even though there might be some convergence among various approaches, implying that "serious alternatives to GDP are around the corner" (Fleurbaey, 2009: 1070). It has been argued that they are important, but not because they will be objective (Diener *et al.*, 2009).

However, the new approach to try to integrate non-monetary aspects when telling the story concerning society's development can be understood as an approach informing on elements important to everyday life and, presumably, in the long run society's development (cf. also "Happiness, social relations and feeling of security" in Chapter 4).

Recent years have seen a growing interest in social capital, as mentioned earlier, as well as how to achieve cohesive societies. Social capital, as measured by relation to others, is therefore an example of an indicator that can be used. A problem with some social indicators is that they focus on individuals' subjective understanding of their lives, for example, whether they can make ends meet. This might be a problem even if someone, who from an objective point of view is a rich or relatively rich person, argues that they are not able to make ends meet, or declares themselves to be living in poverty. However, this can also be argued as a problem when measuring trust, anxiety and happiness. Still, individuals' perception of their lives is an important societal indicator, as was discussed in Chapter 2.

Cohesive societies are seen as more productive societies, and this once again emphasises the need for integrating these aspects when describing society's development.

NEW MEASURE OF SOCIETAL DEVELOPMENT

In Bhutan they have developed a "gross national happiness" index. In most other countries this is not seen as an option as this, perhaps, is too narrowly focused on one aspect of human life. Therefore, efforts could be made to try to integrate more classical understanding of well-being into a new type of index. This is what a British think-tank, the New Economics Foundation (NEF), has done by creating a national account of well-being. This will be described on

p. 107. Also below, there will be a short presentation of the Legatum Prosperity index from another think-thank.

A criticism of these types of index is that they overlook the more traditional aspects such as economic growth and thereby have too little focus on the economic aspects of modern societies although, for example, the Legatum Index combines income and well-being (Legatum Institute, 2010).

New ways of measuring societal development could include a broader variety of indicators. The NEF thus includes personal well-being, social well-being and satisfaction at work. Social well-being is split into supportive relationships and trust and belonging, whereas there is only one indicator for satisfaction at work. Personal well-being will be described below. The data used in the construction of the values in the calculation have been taken from the European Social Survey (see Chapter 3), which used the same survey as the main data-source for the analysis included in this book.

The suggestion from the NEF with regard to personal well-being (see Figure 5.1) is split into five different sections, three of which are further divided. Emotional well-being is divided

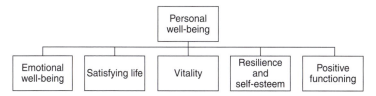

Figure 5.1 Personal well-being and five sub-categories.
Note: Appendix 3 of the report presents the questions related to each of the components described, and thus one component may be based upon several questions. Satisfying life is, for example, based on four questions (NEF, 2008: 21).

into positive feelings and absence of negative feelings, whereas resilience and self-esteem is split into self-esteem, optimism and resilience. Positive functioning has four sub-categories: competence, autonomy, engagement, and meaning and purpose (NEF, 2008). This is not the place for a detailed discussion of each of the components or sub-categories as the main aim is to probe into and indicate that options other than traditional measures are available for the analysis.

The index calculated showed Denmark, Switzerland and Norway at the top, and Ukraine, Bulgaria and Slovakia at the bottom. In this way, to a high degree, it resembles the results based upon use of the single question on happiness. The question of happiness is in fact included, as two of the questions in relation to emotional well-being are: "Taking all things together, how happy would you say you are?" and "How much of the time during the past week were you happy?" Understood in this way, such an account and measure can give rise to a picture of countries which informs about other aspects than do the classical economic approaches.

However, it can also be criticised for not really integrating economic elements in the analysis, such as the development in income and consumption possibilities, the relation to other countries and the public sector's long-term sustainability. Given the discussion on "welfare" (cf. "Happiness and welfare", Chapter 2), it could therefore be useful to combine these indexes to form a combination where not only subjective elements related to well-being and happiness are included, but also the overall societal economic development. This is further due to the fact that income, at least to a certain level, has an impact on the individual's perception of both daily life and long-term happiness. A rapid change in the economic conditions can also have a negative impact on the individual's level of happiness. The discussion here will be on how to combine the elements. It is largely a normative question of how much weight should be attached to the monetary, and how much to the non-monetary, aspects of the measurements.

Another think-tank approach is the prosperity index. This index combines eight sub-indexes related to the following elements: economy, entrepreneurship and opportunity, governance, education, health, safety and security, personal freedom and social capital. For each of them there is an income and well-being component so, in total, 89 different variables are combined and, it is argued, they all have an impact on economic growth or on personal well-being. Well-being is used synonymously with life satisfaction and happiness and it is argued, as well as touched upon several times in this book, that there is a relation between these elements. In Legatum they combine it another way by arguing that: "material wealth cannot be explained only by economic factors, and happiness cannot be explained only by subjective emotions" (Legatum Institute, 2010: 9). Data for the analysis resemble many of those presented above, and this index is linked by using calculated coefficients to reach a score.

Just to give one example, the economy sub-index is calculated using the following elements in Table 5.1.

Table 5.1 shows the need to combine more classical ways of measuring society's development with new types of indicators. Life satisfaction and happiness thus play a larger role than in more classical portraits of societal development. The results of the analysis place the Nordic countries in Europe, and Australia,

Table 5.1 Elements in a sub-economy index

Income	Well-being
Macroeconomic policies:	
Gross domestic savings	Inflation
Unemployment rate	Gross domestic savings
Inflation	
Foundation for growth:	Economic satisfaction and
Capital per worker	expectations
Market size	Satisfaction with standard of
High-tech exports	living
FDI size and volatility	Adequate food and shelter
	Perceived job availability
	Expectations of the economy
	5-year rate of growth
Financial sector efficiency:	
Non-performing loans	Confidence in financial
	institutions

Source: Legatum Institute, 2010, p. 27.

New Zealand and Canada at the top. At the bottom of the 110 countries involved in the analysis are Zimbabwe, Pakistan and the Central African Republic. African countries in general are placed at the bottom of the ranking.

Even though criticism can be made with regard to the way this is done, it is a clear indicator that new ways of understanding and measuring the development of welfare states are important given that the classical approaches only present one picture – albeit an important picture – of the development. A core problem can be the many and varied data – and also the validity of data, at least in some countries, might not be very high.

SUMMING UP

The use of classical economic measurement is not sufficient to inform us about welfare development, nor about a society's sustainability. GDP has several flaws and problems related not only to how it measures income and wealth, but also what is not included, such as personal relations and work in the household, and the reduction in long-term economic and ecological sustainability. At the same time, there often seems to be a good relation between economic development and many subjective indicators of well-being. Measurement of average income and wealth informs neither about the distributional outcome nor about the more complex elements in the measurements.

Therefore, it could be important to develop new combined indexes where one is not only trying to depict and show how the present day appears by economic indicators, but which should also include people's perception and understanding of their happiness. The argument from a utilitarian approach that the outcome of the market alone is best to inform us on people's happiness is thus not precise enough. We need to include a more balanced and more precise measure to be sure we know what will indicate a better life not only in the short term, but also in the long run.

However, there is also a risk that new indexes will become so complicated and detailed that one will fail to see the wood for the trees. The implication of this is that the use of data on happiness can be a simple and relatively precise instrument and a good supplement to the classical economic data on development.

6

CONCLUSIONS

INTRODUCTION

This chapter will sum up the presentation and show how to describe and understand the developments in recent years in research and knowledge on happiness. It will conclude by arguing that studies of happiness are important for the development of the good society, how the concept can be used to increase our knowledge in central social sciences disciplines, and how they can then better enable us to understand present-day societies. It will also highlight what might still be missing in the analysis and use of the concept of happiness.

For many researchers and people in societies, it has often been seen as problematic to ask about happiness. The argument goes that it is the precise choice of the individuals that shows how their lives are and what is best for those individuals, and by adding these elements together this shows, for a libertarian, how a higher level of happiness can be achieved. This seems, however, not to be the case.

WHAT DO WE KNOW?

We know that in several areas there is a clear relation between happiness and the central and important aspects of the development of welfare states. A happy person will often be a person who is employed, married, religious, has good social relations, and is an optimistic person who also trusts other people. The size and impact varies among countries given their historical and institutional structure.

We do know that income has an impact, at least until reaching a certain level, and happy people are healthier and live longer. We also know that winning will only imply a short-term increase in the level of happiness.

People are in fact able to respond to how they understand not only the short-term level of happiness, but also the long-term. The implication is, for example, that even if a person has had an accident, been sick or lost a spouse – although this has a negative impact on their actual level of happiness – it is possible to return to a previous level, or at least rather close to it, and to reflect on happiness over the lifetime as well. This helps in explaining why happiness and age in most analysis is U-shaped – highest when either young or elderly (although for different reasons).

In most welfare state systems having a job is important for the level of happiness, although working more hours might be negative for the individual's level of happiness. This depends on a country's economic performance. People prefer to have something to wake up to and do, and for many this therefore probably implies having a job. Given the impact of education on participation in society and the increase in the possibility of having a job, a higher level of education and life-long learning can be central elements needing to be developed if a society wishes to increase happiness; although free time, including time with family and friends, is very important for many people.

Trust in other people and the political system, and having good social relations, can be seen as central for the level of happiness for many people. Being active in voluntary work, and by this often having good social relations, increases the level of happiness. It might not be the voluntary work in itself which increases happiness, but doing it gives the individual social relations and contact with others.

More equal societies are in most analyses happier than less-equal societies. However, this does not inform us about what the exact level of equality should be, compared with the debate on equality and how individuals react to incentives to perform more and better for societies. However, given the analyses, policy makers wanting a happier society should think about how to achieve more equality without losing efficiency. Whether this also implies a need for equality in happiness is less clear from the analysis.

Social policies and welfare states play a role for the level of happiness. Therefore, if policy makers want a happier nation they will have to look into the role of the welfare state. This can include, among other things, income security, ensuring jobs, a high degree of equality, a good health system, stable governance and a trusting and cohesive society.

Policy makers can use happiness research as a guide besides classical measures of effectiveness, so that if, for example, two types of intervention have the same cost effectiveness, they may choose the one which gives the best improvement in the level of happiness. Sometimes, if happiness is high on the societal list of priorities, it could be that interventions improving happiness can be important. A good example can be that the ability to walk safely in the street at night could require a need for more police on the street, even though from an economic perspective it is not efficient. A problem might be that, as will be expanded in the next section, we do not always know what makes people happier and especially when they have to choose between different types of intervention. Furthermore, a way to establish the possible options and inform individuals is important.

WHAT DO WE NEED TO KNOW MORE ABOUT?

A core problem for research in happiness is that the causal relation is not always clear. This can be questioned in many different areas. Are happier people more likely to live healthily and get a job, or is it the other way round? Do happy people tend to be more extrovert and thereby have more social relations or, again, is it the other way round?

This is clearly among the questions one needs to know more about to ensure that policy advice based upon happiness research is balanced between what has an impact on happiness and what are the results of other types of relations. The possible trade-off between different aspects of happiness and societal development needs to be explored further.

We need to know more about how to avoid the risk of the hedonic treadmill, where even if something is improved there will be a constant quest for better and more goods and services. Or to put it another way around, will a policy for more happiness be doomed because even if it is briefly improved it will drop back if there is no further increase in income or different types of goods and services? How one can sustain happiness is thus also still an open question.

SUMMING UP

Knowledge of what makes people happier can be very important and central for societal development. We need, at the least, some constant new information and updates on elements not covered in traditional economic analysis and data – such as GDP, inflation and unemployment levels – if we are to be able to judge a society's welfare development.

Happiness and happiness research can help to bridge the gap arising from the more classical economic approach to welfare. Understanding of what creates happiness, as indicated in "What do we know?" above, is a start in trying to show what can be important in societal development.

When, for example, we have the knowledge that happiness improves health and that happy people live longer, this might imply a win-win situation both for public sector expenditure and private household economy. Reducing unemployment is another example of a win-win; it will improve the society's economy and will also improve the level of happiness. At the same time there is presumably not a need for an increase in the time people spend at work.

Happiness and research into happiness is here to stay. Economic, sociological, philosophical and psychological studies have for centuries, in some instances, been interested in what creates a good society, and a good society is often seen as a happy society. Knowledge on happiness opens the way for other types of understanding of why individuals and societies reach a specific level of happiness as they do, including how this develops. If we can become happier, sometimes even just for a short while, we might choose this solution instead of a rational decision based on a long-term perspective. The quest for happiness will undoubtedly continue, and the way states, markets and civil society can help in the accomplishment of happiness will therefore always be important.

REFERENCES

Alesina, A., Tellab, R. and MacCulloch, R. (2004), Inequality and happiness: are Europeans and Americans different? *Journal of Public Economics*, 88: 2009–2042.

Allardt, E. (1977), On the relationship between objective and subjective predicaments. *Research Reports, No. 16*. Helsinki: Research Group for Comparative Sociology, University of Helsinki.

Allardt, E. (2003), Den sociala rapporteringens tidstypiska förankring. *Working Paper 14*. Bergen: Stein Rokkan Centre for Social Studies.

Anand, P. and Clark, A. (2006), Symposium introduction: life satisfaction and welfare economics. *The Journal of Socio-Economics*, 35: 177–179.

Argyle, M. (1987), *The Psychology of Happiness*. New York: Methuen.

Argyle, M. (1999), "Causes and correlates of happiness", in D. Kahneman, E. Diener and N. Schwarz (eds) *Well-Being: The foundations of hedonic psychology*. New York: Russell Sage Foundation, pp. 353–373.

Argyle, M. (2001), *The Psychology of Happiness*. London and New York: Routledge.

Argyle, M. and Martin, M. (1991), "The psychological causes of happiness", in F. Strack, M. Argyle and N. Schwarz, *Subjective Well-Being*. Oxford: Pergamon Press.

Aristotle (2000), *Nicomachean Ethics* (translated and edited by Roger Crisp). Cambridge texts in the history of philosophy series. Cambridge, UK/New York: Cambridge University Press.

Arrow, K. J. (1950), A difficulty in the concept of social welfare. *The Journal of Political Economy*, 58(4): 328–346.

Barr, N. (2001), *The Welfare State as Piggy Bank. Information, risk, uncertainty and the role of the state*. Oxford: Oxford University Press.

Berg, M. and Veenhoven, R. (2010), Income inequality and happiness in 119 nations: in search for an optimum that does not exist. Chapter 11 in Greve, B. (ed.) (2010).

Beshears, J. *et al.* (2008), How are preferences revealed? *Journal of Public Economics*, 92: 1787–1794.

Bjørnskov, C., Dreher, A. and Fischer, J. (2007a), The bigger the better? Evidence of government size of life satisfaction around the world. *Public Choice*, 130: 267–292.

Bjørnskov, C., Gupta, N. D. and Pedersen, P. J. (2007b), Analysing trends in subjective well-being in 15 European countries, 1973–2002. *Journal of Happiness Studies*, 9: 317–330.

Blanchflower, D. and Oswald, A. (2004), Well-being over time in Britain and the USA. *Journal of Public Economics*, 88(7–8): 1359–1386.

Blanchflower, D. and Oswald, A (2008), Hypertension and happiness across nations. *Journal of Health Economics*, 27(2): 218–233.

Boarini, R., Johansson, A. and Mira d'Ercole, A. (2006), Alternative measures of well-being. *OECD Economics Department Working Papers, No. 476*. Paris, OECD.

Bok, D. (2010), *The Politics of Happiness. What government can learn from the new research on well-being.* Princeton, NJ and Oxford, UK: Princeton University Press.

Brülde, B. and Bykvist, K. (2010), Happiness, ethics, and politics: introduction, history and conceptual framework. *Journal of Happiness Studies*.

Bruni, L. and Stanca, L. (2008), Watching alone: relational goods, television and happiness. *Journal of Economic Behavior and Organization*, 65(3–4): 506–528.

Caporale, G. M., Georgellis, Y., Tsitsianis, N. and Ya Ping Yin (2007), Income and happiness across Europe: do reference values matter? *CESifo Working Paper, No. 2146*. Munich.

Clapham, D. (2010), Happiness, well-being and housing policy. *Policy & Politics*, 38(2): 253–267.

Clark, A. E. (2007), Born to be mild? Cohort effects don't (fully) explain why well-being is U-shaped in age. *IZA Working Paper, No. 3170*.

Clark, A. E. and Oswald, A. J. (2002), A simple statistical method for measuring how life events affect happiness. *International Journal of Epidemiology*, 31: 1139–1144.

Clark, A. E., Frijters, P. and Shields, M. A. (2008), Relative income, happiness, and utility: an explanation for the Easterlin Paradox and other puzzles. *Journal of Economic Literature*, 46(1): 95–144.

Coleman, J. (1988), Social capital in the creation of human capital. *Journal of Sociology*, 94: 95–120.

Cullis, J., Hudson, J. and Jones, P. (2010), A different rationale for redistribution: pursuit of happiness in the European Union. *Journal of Happiness Studies*.

Danner, D., Snowdon, D. and Friesen, W. (2001), Positive emotions in early life and longevity: findings from the Nun Study. *Journal of Personality and Social Psychology*, 80(5): 804–813.

Delamothe, T. (2005), Happiness. Get happy – it's good for you. *BMJ*, 331: 1489–1490.

Diener, E. and Seligman, M. (2004), Beyond money. Toward an economy of well-being. *Psychological Science in the Public Interest*, 5(1): 1–31.

Diener, E., Sandvik, E., Seidlitz, L. and Diener, M. (1997), Recent findings on subjective well-being. *Indian Journal of Clinical Psychology*, 24(1): 25–41.

Diener, E., Suh, E. M., Lucas, R. E. and Smith, H. L. (1999), Subjective wellbeing: three decades of progress. *Psychological Bulletin*, 125(2): 276–303.

Diener, E., Lucas, R., Schimmack, U. and Helliwell, J. (2009), *Well-being for Public Policy*. Oxford: Oxford University Press.

Duncan, G. (2005), What do we mean by "Happiness"? The relevance of subjective well-being to social policy. *Social Policy Journal of New Zealand*, 25: 16–31.

Duncan, G. (2010), Should happiness-maximization be the goal of government? *Journal of Happiness Studies*, 11: 163–178.

Durayappah, Adorée (2010), The 3P model: a general theory of subjective well-being. *Journal of Happiness Studies*.

Easterlin, R. A. (1995), Will raising the income of all increase the happiness of all? *Journal of Economic Behavior and Organization*, 27: 35–47.

Easterlin, R. A. (2001), Income and happiness: towards a unified theory. *The Economic Journal*, 111: 465–484.

ESS Round 3, Jowell, R. and the Central Co-ordinating Team (2007), *European Social Survey 2006/2007: Technical Report.* London: Centre for Comparative Social Surveys, City University.

European Commission (2009), *The Social Situation in the European Union 2008.* Brussels: European Commission.

European Foundation for the Improvement of Living and Working Conditions (2003), *First European Quality of Life Survey: Life satisfaction, happiness and sense of belonging.* Dublin: Eurofound, www.eurofound.eu.int.

European Foundation for the Improvement of Living and Working Conditions (2004a), *Quality of Life in Europe. Resumé.* Dublin: Eurofound, www.eurofound.eu.int.

European Foundation for the Improvement of Living and Working Conditions (2004b), *Quality of life in Europe: an illustrative report. Summary.* Dublin: Eurofound, www.eurofound.eu.int.

Field, J. (2008), *Social Capital.* London and New York: Routledge.

Field, J. (2009), Well-being and happiness. *IFLL Thematic Paper 4.* Leicester: NIACE.

Fischer, J. (2009), Happiness and age cycles – return to start? On the functional relationship between subjective well-being and age. *OECD Social, Employment and Migration Working Papers, No. 99.* Paris: OECD.

Fleurbaey, M. (2009), Beyond GDP: the quest for a measure of social welfare. *Journal of Economic Literature,* 47(4): 1029–1075.

Fors, F. (2010), Happiness in the extensive welfare state: Sweden in a comparative European perspective. In Greve, B. (ed.), 2010.

Frey, B. S. and Stutzer, A. (2002a), What can economists learn from happiness research? *Journal of Economic Literature,* XL(2): 402–435.

Frey, B. S. and Stutzer, A (2002b), *Happiness and Economics. How the economy and institutions affect well-being.* Princeton, NJ: Princeton University Press.

Goerne, A. (2010), The capability approach in social policy analysis. Yet another concept? *Recwowe Working Paper on the Reconciliation of work and welfare in Europe.* University of Edinburgh.

Graham, C. (2008), Happiness and health: lessons – and questions – for public policy. *Health Affairs,* 27(1): 72–87.

Graham, C. (2009), *Happiness around the World: The paradox of happy peasants and miserable millionaires.* Oxford: Oxford University Press.

Greve, B. (2008), What is welfare? *Central European Journal of Public Policy*, 2(1): 52–75.

Greve, B. (2009), Can choice in welfare states be equitable? *Social Policy & Administration*, 43(6): 543–556.

Greve, B. (ed.) (2010), *Happiness and Social Policy in Europe.* Cheltenham: Edward Elgar.

Haidt, J. (2006), *The Happiness Hypothesis.* London: Arrow Books.

Haidt, J., Seder, P. and Kesebir, S. (2008), Hive psychology, happiness, and public policy. *Journal of Legal Studies*, 37: 133–156.

Helliwell, J. (2003), How's life? Combining individual and national variables to explain subjective well-being. *Economic Modelling*, 20(2): 331–360.

Hirsch, F. (1977), *Social Limits to Growth.* London: Routledge.

Ho, Lok Sang (2010), *Happiness and Public Policy.* Economics Department and Centre for Public Policy Studies, Lingnan University.

Hoorn, Andre van (2008), A short introduction to subjective well-being: Its measurement, correlates and policy uses. Chapter 15 in OECD (2007) *Statistics, Knowledge and Policy 2007*, Paris: OECD.

Hylland Eriksen, T. (2008), *Jakten på lycka i överflödssamhället.* Nora: Bokförlaget Nya Doxa.

Inglehart, R., Foa, R., Peterson, C. and Welzel, C. (2008), Development, freedom, and rising happiness. *Perspectives on Psychological Science*, 3(4): 264–285.

Johns, H. and Ormerod, P. (2007), *Happiness, Economics and Public Policy.* London: The Institute of Economic Affairs.

Jordan, Bill (2008), *Welfare and Well-being. Social Value in Public Policy.* Bristol: Policy Press.

Kacapyr, E. (2008), Cross-country determinants of satisfaction with life. *International Journal of Social Economics*: 35(6): 400–416.

Kavetsos, G. and Szymanski, S. (2010), National well-being and international sports events. *Journal of Economic Psychology*, 31: 158–171.

Kesebir, P. and Diener, E (2008), In defence of happiness: why policymakers should care about subjective well-being, in L. Bruni, F. Comin, and M. Pugno, *Capabilities and Happiness*. Oxford: Oxford University Press.

Knack, S. (2000), Social capital and the quality of government. Evidence from the United States. *Policy Research Working Paper 2504*. Washington, DC: The World Bank.

Konow, J. and Earley, J. (2008), The hedonistic paradox: is *homo economicus* happier? *Journal of Public Economics*, 92: 1–33.

Köszedi, B. (2008), Choices, situations, and happiness. *Journal of Public Economics*, 92: 1821–1832.

Kroll, C. (2008), *Social Capital and the Happiness of Nations*. Frankfurt am Main: Peter Lang.

Layard, R. (2003), Lionel Robbins Memorial Lectures 2002/3: Happiness. Has social science a clue? RL348b. Delivered on 3–5 March at London School of Economics.

Layard, R. (2005), *Happiness. Lessons from a new science*. London: Penguin.

Layard, R. (2008), Introduction. *Journal of Public Economics*, 92: 1773–1776.

Lee, D. Y., Park, S. H., Uhlemann, M. R. and Patsula, P. (1999), What makes you happy? A comparison of self-reported criteria of happiness between two cultures. *Social Indicators Research*, 50: 351–362.

Legatum Institute (2010), *The 2010 Legatum Prosperity Index*. www.prosperity.com.

Lelkes, O. (2006a), Knowing what is good for you. Empirical analysis of personal preferences and the "objective good". *The Journal of Socio-Economics*, 35: 285–307.

Lelkes, O. (2006b), Tasting Freedom: happiness, religion and economic transition. *Journal of Economic History*, 59: 173–194.

Lelkes, O. (2008), Happiness across the life-cycle: exploring age-specific preferences. *Policy Brief 2, 2008*. Vienna: European Centre.

Leung, A., Jier, C., Fung, T., Fung, L. and Sproule, R. (2010), Searching for happiness: the importance of social capital. *Journal of Happiness Studies*.

Little, I. M. D. (2002), *Ethics, Economics and Politics. Principles of public policy*. Oxford: Oxford University Press.

Loewenstein, G. and Ubel, P. (2008), Hedonic adaptation and the role of decision and experience utility in public policy. *Journal of Public Economics*, 92: 1795–1810.

McMahan, E. and Estes, D. (2010), Measuring lay conceptions of well-being: the beliefs about well-being scale. *Journal of Happiness Studies*.

Mau, S. and Verwiebe, R. (2010), *European Societies. Mapping structure and change*. Bristol: Policy Press.

Myers, D. (2004), *Psychology*. New York: Worth.

NEF (2008), *National Accounts of Well-being: Bringing real wealth onto the balance sheet*. www.nationalaccountsofwellbeing.org.

Nettle, D. (2005), *Happiness. The Science behind your smile*. Oxford: Oxford University Press.

Ng, Y. (2002), The East-Asian happiness gap: speculating on causes and implications, *Pacific Economic Review*, 7(1): 51–63.

Ng, Y. and Ho, L. (eds) (2006), *Happiness and Public Policy: Theory, case studies and implications*. Houndmills: Palgrave Macmillan.

Nordhaus, W. and Tobin, J. (1973), Is growth obsolete? *Cowles Foundation Paper 398*, Yale University, New Haven, CT, pp. 509–564. Reprinted from M. Moss (ed.), The measurement of economic and social performance, studies in income and wealth. *NBER*, 38.

OECD (2005), *Society at a Glance, 2005. OECD Social Indicators*. Paris: OECD.

OECD (2006), *Society at a Glance, 2006*. Paris: OECD.

OECD (2007), *Statistics, Knowledge and Policy 2007: Measuring and fostering the progress of societies*. Paris: OECD.

OECD (2009), *Society at a Glance 2009*. Paris: OECD.

Okulicz-Kozaryn, A. (2010), Europeans work to live and Americans live to work (who is happy to work more: Americans or Europeans?). *Journal of Happiness Studies*.

Oorschot, W. van and Arts, W. (2005), The social capital of European welfare states: the crowding out hypothesis revisited. *Journal of European Social Policy*, 15(1): 5–26.

Oswald, A. J. (1997), Happiness and economic performance. *The Economic Journal*, 107(445): 1815–1831.

Oswald, A. J. and Powdthavee, N. (2006), Does happiness adapt? A longitudinal study of disability with implications for economist and judges. *IZA Discussion Paper, No. 2208*. University of London.

Ott, J. (2005), Level and inequality of happiness in nations: does greater happiness of a greater number imply greater inequality in happiness? *Journal of Happiness Studies*, 6: 397–420.

Ott, J. (2010), Limited experienced happiness or unlimited expected utility, What about the differences? *Journal of Happiness Studies*.

Pacek, A. and Radcliff, B. (2008), Assessing the welfare state: the politics of happiness. *Perspectives on Politics*, 6: 267–277.

Peiro, A. (2006), Happiness, satisfaction and socio-economic conditions: some international evidence. *The Journal of Socio-Economics*, 35: 348–365.

Pollock, F. (1877), Happiness or welfare. *Mind*, 2(6): 269–272.

Post, G. S. (2005), Altruism, happiness and health: it's good to be good. *International Journal of Behavioral Medicine*, 12(2): 66–77.

Prycker, V. (2010), Happiness on the political agenda? PROS and CONS. *Journal of Happiness Studies*, 11(5): 585–603.

Rothstein, B. (2010), Happiness and the welfare state. *Social Research*, 77(2): 1–28.

Rothstein, B. and Stolle, D. (2007), The quality of government and social capital: a theory of political institutions and generalized trust. *QoG Working Paper Series 2007: 2*. Gøteborg University.

Schimmel, J. (2007), Development as happiness: the subjective perception of happiness and UNDP's analysis of poverty, wealth and development. *Journal of Happiness Studies*.

Schumaker, J. F. (2007), *In Search of Happiness. Understanding an endangered state of mind*. London: Praeger.

Schwartz, C. E., Keyl, P. M., Marcum, J. P. and Bod, R. (2008), Helping others shows differential benefits on health and well-being for male and female teens. *Journal of Happiness Studies*, 10(4): 431–448.

Seligman, M. (2002a), *Authentic Happiness. Using the new positive psychology to realize your potential for lasting fulfilment*. New York: Free Press.

Sen, A. (2008), The economics of happiness and capability, in L. Bruni, F. Comin, and M. Pugno (eds), *Capabilities and Happiness*. Oxford: Oxford University Press.

Sen, A. (2009), *The Idea of Justice*. London: Allen Lane.

Slesnick, D. (1998), Empirical approaches to the measurement of welfare. *Journal of Economic Literature*, 36(4): 2108–2165.

Smith, K. (2008), Reflections on the literature. *Review of Environmental Economics and Policy*, 1: 1–17.

Stiglitz, J. E., Sen, A. and Fitoussi, J. P. (eds) (2009), *Report by the Commission on the Measurement of Economic Performance and Social Progress*. Paris: Commission on the Measurement of Economic Performance and Social Progress.

Sumner, L. W. (2003), *Welfare, Happiness, and Ethics*. Oxford: Clarendon Press.

Tella, R. Di and MacCulloch, R. J. (2008), Gross national happiness as an answer to the Easterlin Paradox? *Journal of Development Economics*, 86: 22–42.

Tella, R. Di, MacCulloch, R. J. and Oswald, A. J. (2003), The macro-economics of happiness. *Review of Economics and Statistics*, 85(4): 809–827.

Thaler, R. H. and Sunstein, C. R. (2008), *Nudge. Improving Decisions about Health, Wealth, and Happiness*. New Haven, CT, and London: Yale University Press.

van Praag, B. M. S. (1993) The relativity of the welfare concept, in A. Sen and M. Nussbaum (eds), *Quality of Life*. Oxford: Clarence Press.

Veenhoven, R. (1991), Is happiness relative? *Social Indicators Research*, 24(1): 1–34.

Veenhoven, R. (2008a), False promise of happiness. *Journal of Happiness Studies*, 10: 385–386.

Veenhoven, R. (2008b), Healthy happiness: Effects of happiness on physical health and the consequences for preventive health care. *Journal of Happiness Studies*, 9: 449–469.

Veenhoven, R. (2008c), Measures of gross national happiness. Chapter 16 in OECD (2007), *Statistics, Knowledge and Policy 2007*, Paris: OECD.

Veenhoven, R. (2010), Greater happiness for a greater number. Is that possible and desirable? *Journal of Happiness Studies*, DOI 10.1007/s10902-010-9204-z.

Walker, A. (1997), Whither welfare? in C. Ballard, J. Gubbay, and C. Middleton (eds), *The Student's Companion to Sociology*. Oxford: Blackwell.

Waterman, A., Schwartz, S. and Conti, R. (2008), The implications of two conceptions of happiness (hedonic enjoyment and eudaimonia) for the understanding of intrinsic motivation, *Journal of Happiness Studies*, 9: 41–79.

Weisbach, D. A. (2007), *What Does Happiness Research Tell Us about Taxation?* Chicago, IL: The University of Chicago Law School.

Wilkinson, N. (2008), *An Introduction to Behavioral Economics*. New York: Palgrave Macmillan.

Wilkinson, R. G. (2006), The impact of inequality. *Social Research*, 73(2): ss. 711–732.

Winkelmann, R. (2008), Unemployment, social capital, and subjective well-being. *Journal of Happiness Studies*.

Yang, Y. (2008), Social inequalities in happiness in the United States, 1972 to 2004: An Age-Period-Cohort Analysis. *American Sociological Review*, 73: 204–226.

INDEX